YOU ARE RECEIVING REVELATION

NOW ACT ON IT

LOREN G. DALTON

CFI
An imprint of Cedar Fort, Inc.
Springville, Utah

What others are saying about this book

"This is simply the most practical guide I have ever come across for how—really how—to recognize and act upon the promptings of the Spirit. I have story after story of how following this approach has been life-changing for me personally. This is a life-changing book. It's as simple as that."

—Greg McKeown, podcaster and *New York Times* best-selling author of *Effortless* and *Essentialism*

"How can we better recognize the promptings of the Spirit? Can we learn to receive revelation? Loren Dalton does a masterful job helping us understand and answer these important questions. This is a much-needed book. I'm grateful that he wrote it, and I highly recommend it."

—Jane Clayson Johnson, journalist and best-selling author of *Silent Souls Weeping* and *I Am a Mother*

"Loren's take on personal revelation couldn't have come at a better time. In our chaotic world, I often wonder which thoughts are mine and which are divine. Blending inspiring examples and true doctrine, Loren gives us spiritual tools we can use every day to act with greater faith. Some books are timely, some are timeless. This is both."

—Jason Wright, *New York Times* best-selling author, creator, speaker

"If you are looking for inspiration about inspiration, then this is the book for you. Loren writes with clarity, using vivid stories, easy to comprehend instructions, and insights that are immediately actionable. The world has deep need for more goodness and light. Go build the kingdom of God today—now—by learning to recognize and act on the regular inspiration flowing from God to you through the Holy Ghost. This book will help."

—Taylor Halverson, PhD, gospel scholar

"When someone is able to frame a gospel principle like following the Spirit in an applicable way, we are able to take action right away and see the difference the gospel makes in our lives. Loren Dalton does exactly that in this inspiring book. All should read it and consider how the Spirit is prompting them today."

—Kurt Francom
Host of *Leading Saints* podcast

"We are all looking to better understand how to receive personal revelation to guide our lives. Brother Dalton takes this important gospel principle and brings practical application on how to make this real in each of our lives. He also helps us understand how to discern between personal revelation from our Heavenly Father and the subtle, but constant whispers from the adversary. I encourage everyone to read this book."

—Richard Ostler, author of
Listen, Learn, and Love series

ISBN 13: 978-1-4621-4513-3

Published by CFI, an imprint of Cedar Fort, Inc.
2373 W. 700 S., Suite 100, Springville, UT 84663
Distributed by Cedar Fort, Inc., www.cedarfort.com

Library of Congress Control Number: 2022950905

Cover design by Shawnda T. Craig

Printed in the United States of America

10 9 8 7 6 5 4 3 2 1

Printed on acid-free paper

To my eternal companion, Annette

You are the love of my life and a comfort and joy to my soul!
Thank you for always believing in me!
You make me look forward to the eternities!

CONTENTS

SECTION THREE
The Adventure Begins!

ACKNOWLEDGMENTS

I owe more than I can express to my wonderful parents, Leonard Franklynn Dalton and Davida Payne Dalton. They had eleven children and sixty-nine grandchildren and did an amazing job of raising us to love the Lord. They left a legacy of love and belief in the gospel of Jesus Christ. Many of the things taught in this book, I first learned from my angel mother! I have never known anyone personally who was as close to the Savior as she was.

Even when it seemed that nobody else did, my eternal sweetheart, Annette, always believed in me and in the person I could become. That belief and support has carried me through some very difficult times and helped me accomplish more than I could have dreamed on my own. I don't think she understands just how much she has done and continues to do to help me grow. I love and appreciate her with all I have.

I owe a huge debt of gratitude to my younger sister, JoEllen Dalton Johnson. Besides Annette, I don't think anyone has been a bigger cheerleader for me in getting this book published than JoEllen. She has also served as the editor of my manuscript. She went over every word of this book a few different times and made it so much better. I can't thank her enough. I am also grateful for each of my other nine siblings. Some of them have stories in this book. I love each one of them dearly and am grateful for the positive influence they have been in my life.

In addition, I would like to thank my amazingly talented and brilliant niece, Danielle Carter. Danielle did the entire bibliography of this book for me. I can't imagine all of the work she needed to put in to get this done, but I will never be able to thank her enough for the professional and thorough job that she did.

I am also very grateful to my daughter Colette Dalton, who got me started on this journey by getting me an invitation to speak at a devotional for what was then known as the LDS Business College (now Ensign College). That talk became fairly popular on the internet, and it was in response to that talk that people began asking me to write a book on the subject. I am truly grateful for the wonderful love and support of my other three children and their spouses as well: Michael and Kyley Dalton, Tyler and Aubrey Sharp, and Jenna Dalton. We are so grateful for such wonderful children (and their spouses and children). What joy they bring to our lives.

This book would probably not have been published had it not been for national best-selling author Greg McKeown. He reached out to me after seeing my devotional talk. It was not long after I had been rejected by three different publishers and was looking to try to self-publish. He looked over my manuscript and gave me some invaluable counsel. In following his advice, my very next submission was a success! I can't thank him enough for his amazing help and insight.

Finally, I want to thank each of our wonderful missionaries in the Brazil São Paulo Interlagos Mission. Their questions and concerns as they worried about not getting promptings from the Spirit were what led me to begin putting these principles into a form that could be shared and taught to them and others. I love those missionaries as if they were my own children and will forever be grateful that the Lord had the confidence in Annette and me to oversee their efforts in the Lord's work for those three glorious years that we were able to serve with them. I pray for each of them daily! I am also grateful for the wonderful missionaries and counselors with whom I was blessed to serve in the California Sacramento Mission and the Utah Orem Mission—and especially the wonderful leadership and mentorship of the four mission presidents with whom I served, namely R. Craig Hansen, R. Randall Huff, James S. Jardine, and Gordon L. Treadway. I am eternally grateful for Wilford A. Cardon and John H. Hawkins (my two mission presidents with whom I served as a young man and the two men who—besides my father—had the greatest impact on my life). They will never know all they did for me and for my future in the short time that I was blessed to serve under them as a missionary in Brazil.

INTRODUCTION

"As a spirit being, He [the Holy Ghost] has the unique responsibility of being an agent through which personal revelation is received."

—Elder Craig C. Christensen[1]

How many times have you wished you knew how to receive personal revelation? You know what I'm talking about. You have been sitting in a sacrament meeting, watching general conference, or even just listening to other people talk. And you hear about someone getting a revelation to do something or to not do something. When you hear this, you wonder what is wrong with you. You have lived a good life and have tried to make right choices. So, why does this never happen to you? Did you do something that "kicked you out of the 'club'"? Why can't you ever get a revelation like everyone else around you?

You're not alone! I suspect that a good majority of members of the Church have had these same feelings and have been filled with the same doubts about themselves. Worse still, some very good people have left the Church, believing that because they were sure that they never had any revelations, they were too unworthy to be in the Church, and they just gave up. Others have fasted and prayed for two days straight, not wanting to stop until they had received a revelation, only to quit without having had the experience they were looking for.

If you are like many members, you have felt an even more urgent need to figure out how to receive personal revelation with President Nelson's oft-quoted statement that "in coming days, it will not be

---

1. Christensen, "Unspeakable Gift from God," 13.

possible to survive spiritually without the guiding, directing, comforting, and constant influence of the Holy Ghost."[2]

This book is for YOU—you who represent the majority of Church members but who feel that you are all alone with this challenge. People don't talk about it much (not wanting to admit that they don't get revelations, when it seems everyone around them is). Unfortunately, because of this, you don't know that many people feel just like you. If you have felt that you were one of the only active members of the Church who had not received any revelation, you will be excited to turn each page of this book.

This book pulls back the curtain on the mysteries of how any individual member of the Church can recognize revelation. It does the same with how to recognize when the adversary is talking to you, as well. Are these things you have always wanted to know? Then let's get started! I hope you will find this book to be a huge help for you as you live your life. And, as a result, you will end up blessing the lives of many others.

2. Nelson, "Revelation for Our Lives," 96.

SECTION ONE

The First *Bing!*

CHAPTER 1

Why Don't I Get Promptings from the Holy Ghost?

"The ability to qualify for, receive, and act on personal revelation is the single most important skill that can be acquired in this life."

—Sister Julie B. Beck[1]

I wrote this book with two goals in mind, namely, that each reader of this book will (1) realize that you are indeed receiving revelation on a constant basis, and (2) commit to act immediately on the revelations you receive.

Joseph Smith said, "The Holy Ghost is a revelator."[2] More specifically, he said, "**No man can receive the Holy Ghost without receiving revelations**."[3]

In reading this, I know some of you are thinking, "Well, what does that say about me? I have never had a revelation! Does that mean, even though I was confirmed a member and was told to receive the Holy Ghost, that, in fact, I never actually did receive Him into my life? And if not, why not? What is wrong with me?"

In as emphatically of a way as I can possibly write this response, I want to tell you that **THERE IS NOTHING WRONG WITH YOU!** And, if you think you have not ever had a revelation, I want to

1. Beck, "Upon the Handmaids," 11.
2. Smith, Joseph, Teachings of the Prophet, 339.
3. Smith, Joseph, Teachings of the Prophet, 339; emphasis added.

tell you that **YOU ARE WRONG!** You *have* been receiving revelations. You just haven't recognized that you have been receiving them. Allow me to explain.

My "Awakening" in Brazil

It was June 27, 2014. My wife, Annette, and I had just landed at the Guarulhos Airport in São Paulo, Brazil. We were moving there (along with our youngest daughter, Jenna) to begin our three-year term of service as mission president and companion of the Brazil São Paulo Interlagos Mission. Pacheco Pinho and his wife, Bia, picked us up at the airport. The Pinhos were just completing their three years of service, and they had done an amazing job. We received an outstanding mission from them, full of obedient and hardworking missionaries. President Pinho had done such a masterful job as mission president that I felt nervous about following such a great leader. In my career, I had usually inherited challenges—"turnaround" situations where I was called on to "fix" a broken situation. But this mission was doing amazingly well. What more could I do in following such a great leader? To be honest, I just didn't want to mess things up.

Upon our arrival in the mission home, I began prayerfully considering what my first message to our missionaries should be. I knew that we would soon be gathering for zone conferences throughout the mission so my wife and I could introduce ourselves to all of our missionaries as their new mission president and companion. I had already written a "first talk" for the mission that I had brought with me, but I was now having a strong feeling that I shouldn't give that talk. Instead, I felt impressed that there were three messages I needed to share with the missionaries:

1. **Don't worry—I don't want to change anything.** I wanted them to continue being the great, obedient, and hardworking missionaries that the Pinhos had trained them to be. I knew that they loved their previous mission president and were probably a bit skeptical about this new guy who was coming in to take his place and about the changes I would make. I didn't want to make changes from what he had done (certainly not

right away), and I didn't want the missionaries to worry about that. I wanted them to know that I loved and respected their president.

2. **"Begin with the end in mind":** This was the title of the strong message delivered to us from then-Elder Russell M. Nelson in the New Mission Presidents' Seminar that we had attended just prior to leaving for Brazil (in late June 2014). His point was that we should always help our missionaries have a strong and constant focus on the temple in our work—from their earliest stages of contact and teaching with each family and individual that our missionaries taught and continue past baptism. I loved this message. The Lord confirmed to me that this needed to be a theme in our mission. As a result, the temple ended up being a major focus in our mission.
3. **Follow the promptings of the Holy Ghost:** Instead of working on plan A or plan B, I wanted them to follow plan C. I wanted to help them see that plan C (the celestial plan) was to do what *God* wants them to do each day. Instead of focusing on what *we* think would be best to do that day, if we would just seek and follow His promptings about where to go and what to do, we would have much better results. Obviously, He won't always tell us. For that reason, it is still important to have our plans made out (plans A and B). However, if we always ask, we will be in a better position to hear and act on His promptings. In doing this daily, we would be much more successful as missionaries.

Following my strong impressions to focus on those three items, I completely rewrote my talk and headed off to our first zone conferences. At the conclusion of those first conferences, I felt that they had gone very well. Other than my rusty Portuguese, I remember feeling very good about having focused my remarks on those three important areas. However, over the next couple of weeks, several missionaries asked to meet with me. At first, I was excited. I hoped that this meant that my first talk had resonated with them and that we were going to build strong relationships and really start taking off in the work. Then, the reality set in. Many of those interviews were missionaries coming to me heartbroken, with tears in their eyes. One missionary after another "confessed" to me that they had never received a revelation or even a prompting from the Holy Ghost and that they felt that they wouldn't be able to accomplish my request to focus on plan C. They wanted to know what was wrong with them as missionaries—or even as Christians. It hurt me so much to see them feel this way!

At that point, I knew why God had inspired me to change my talk and to make sure that I talked about following His promptings. It hit me like a ton of bricks. In my first message to the missionaries, I helped wake them up to what they wanted: to feel the promptings of the Spirit. These amazing and worthy young men and women had been taught for years—or, in many cases, only months, since we had several missionaries who were very recent converts—to follow the promptings of the Holy Ghost, but they had never been taught *how* to recognize those promptings when they came. In fact, it struck me that this wasn't something that has been taught very clearly to the members of the Church as a whole. As a result, although these great missionaries had been getting promptings, they had not been recognizing that they had been getting them. And, since they didn't recognize that they had been getting them, they felt terrible about themselves because they thought they had never gotten any promptings. They worried that perhaps they had never been fully forgiven for past transgressions or, for some other reason, the Lord had deemed them unworthy to receive promptings. It was my responsibility as their mission president to teach them that they were, indeed, receiving revelations and how, in the future, they could recognize these promptings when they would get them.

Over the next several months, I began teaching our wonderful missionaries how to recognize the promptings of the Holy Ghost when they received them. And I *retaught* this same message for the rest of my mission, not only because I was always getting new missionaries who did not understand these principles, but also because I felt it very important to reinforce the message to those missionaries who had heard it from me previously. Many of these outstanding missionaries shared with me that learning how to recognize the promptings, or whisperings, of the Holy Ghost completely changed their missions and would forever change their lives!

I also felt that I needed to reach out and teach these same principles to the members, as well. I taught these principles in stake conference addresses to every stake in our mission in Brazil. And I have taught it in many talks that I have been asked to give since returning to the States after our mission. And now, with the encouragement of many people who have heard my message on this subject, I have been impressed to put these same principles on this matter into a book so that this important message can be shared with even more people.

The messages we have heard from our dear prophet, Russell M. Nelson, since he became prophet have only reinforced to me the importance of writing this book. He has shared many different messages about the Holy Ghost and the importance for us to receive and act on revelation. Not only do we remember his promise about the "coming days" (quoted in the introduction of this book), but he has also said, "My beloved brothers and sisters, I plead with you to increase your spiritual capacity to receive revelation."[4]

From these words and others from him (and other Church leaders), we *know* that it is important to follow the promptings of the Holy Ghost. However, as I experienced with my missionaries in Brazil, we don't hear very often about *how* to recognize His promptings when they come to us. Knowing that members want to follow the prophet, I felt that this message about how to recognize the promptings from the Spirit was a message that needed to be written down in book form. I want to help as many members as possible better understand how to recognize the promptings from the Holy Ghost and be committed to act immediately on all promptings when they come. In addition, in this book you will learn how to recognize the very deceptive promptings of the adversary, so that you will no longer be deceived by him and accidentally follow his promptings.

Have You Accepted the Gift of the Holy Ghost?

Wilford Woodruff, one of the early prophets and presidents of The Church of Jesus Christ of Latter-day Saints, said, "You may have the administration of angels; you may see many miracles; you may

4. Russell M. Nelson, "Revelation for the Church, Revelation for Our Lives."

see many wonders in the earth; but I claim that **the gift of the Holy Ghost is the greatest gift that can be bestowed upon man.**"[5] What a bold statement. This same message has been reiterated by many prophets throughout the years.

Knowing that it is the greatest gift we can have, shouldn't this scripture from the Doctrine and Covenants take on new meaning for us? "For what doth it profit a man if a gift is bestowed upon him, and he receive not the gift? Behold, he rejoices not in that which is given unto him, neither rejoices in him who is the giver of the gift" (Doctrine and Covenants 88:33). So, even though it is the greatest gift that can be bestowed upon us, that means nothing to us unless and until we do all we can to accept the gift and then work to keep it with us at all times.

LeGrand Richards, a great Apostle in the Church whom I remember from my childhood, put it this way: "To me, the gift of the Holy Ghost is as important to man as sunshine and water are to the plants. You take them away, and the plants would die. You take the Holy Ghost out of this Church, and this Church would not be any different than any other church."[6]

So, if it is the greatest gift we can get—and the thing that most distinguishes us from other religions—why do we not understand it very well? My theory is this: Of all the gifts of God to His children, doesn't it make sense that His *greatest* gift to us would be the one the adversary would *least* want us to comprehend? Satan has worked very hard at getting us to downplay and misunderstand this most miraculous of gifts.

Who Can Feel the Influence of the Holy Ghost?

On more than one occasion, I have had a confused member or missionary tell me that they heard of a non-member friend or relative who had a prompting from the Holy Ghost. They wondered how this was possible, since that person had not been baptized nor received the gift of the Holy Ghost. We should not be surprised by this at all. It is

5. Woodruff, "March 5th, 1889"; emphasis added
6. Richards, "The Gift," 76.

important to note that having the influence of the Holy Ghost is *not* something that has only been given to baptized and confirmed members of The Church of Jesus Christ of Latter-day Saints. This blessing is for all of God's children. It is especially beneficial for those honest seekers of truth. **If non-members could not feel the influence of the Holy Ghost, there would indeed be very few converts to the gospel of Jesus Christ.** The way that they join the Church is that the Holy Ghost testifies to them of the truthfulness of what the missionaries are teaching them. The Holy Ghost is the greatest missionary in the world. Every returned missionary can share many different stories of how the Holy Ghost touched someone that they were teaching in a very special way on their path toward making their baptismal covenant with Heavenly Father. Not all of those people followed through and were baptized, but the Holy Ghost was (and is) constantly doing his part.

Joseph Smith taught that the Holy Ghost and revelations are open to all who follow the same principles. He once said, "It is the privilege of the children of God to come to God and get revelation. . . . God is not a respecter of persons; we all have the same privilege."[7]

The Influence Versus the Gift of the Holy Ghost

If every child of God on earth, member of the Church or not, can have the blessings of being influenced by the Holy Ghost, why is it so important to receive the Holy Ghost after baptism? Joseph Smith taught, "There is a difference between the Holy Ghost and the gift of the Holy Ghost. Cornelius received the Holy Ghost before he was baptized, which was the convincing power of God unto him of the truth of the Gospel, but he could not receive the *gift* of the Holy Ghost until after he was baptized. Had he not taken this sign or ordinance upon him, the Holy Ghost which convinced him of the truth of God, would have left him."[8]

President Dallin H. Oaks gave a great example of this difference, as expressed by a recent convert:

---

7. Richards, Pocket Companion, 75; 78–79.
8. Smith, Joseph, *Teachings of the Prophet*, 204; emphasis added.

> A newly baptized member told me what she felt when she received that gift. This was a faithful Christian woman who had spent her life in service to others. She knew and loved the Lord, and she had felt the manifestations of his Spirit. When she received the added light of the restored gospel, she was baptized and the elders placed their hands upon her head and gave her the gift of the Holy Ghost. She recalled, "I felt the influence of the Holy Ghost settle upon me with greater intensity than I had ever felt before. He was like an old friend who had guided me in the past but now had come to stay."[9]

I love this story. As with the example of Cornelius, it teaches us that the beautiful influence of the Holy Ghost is open to everyone. However, the constant companionship of the Holy Ghost is that great gift we are given the opportunity to receive *after we are baptized* by someone who has the proper authority. And it will only stay with us as long as we remain worthy.

Who Was Right—Joseph Smith or Russell M. Nelson?

As we stated at the beginning of this chapter, Joseph Smith taught, "**No man can receive the Holy Ghost without receiving revelations.** The Holy Ghost is a revelator."[10] However, President Nelson told us in the April 2018 general conference that "if we are to have any hope of sifting through the myriad of voices and the philosophies of men that attack truth, **we must learn to receive revelation**."[11]

In reading these two quotes—one from our first prophet of the Restoration and the other from our most recent living prophet—one could easily feel that they are contradictory in nature. Joseph says that you cannot get the Holy Ghost without getting revelations, and President Nelson tells us that we need to "learn to receive revelation." In reality, the words of these two great prophets are not at odds with each other at all; in fact, their messages actually support one another.

9. Oaks, "Always Have His Spirit," 60.
10. Smith, Joseph, *Teachings of the Prophet*, 339; emphasis added.
11. Nelson, "Revelation for Our Lives," 96; emphasis added.

They were simply talking about two different responsibilities when it comes to receiving revelation.

Joseph was talking about the role and responsibility of the Holy Ghost. His quote clearly states that the Holy Ghost is a revelator. As such, he says that by receiving the Holy Ghost, we automatically receive revelations because that is who the Holy Ghost is and what He does. In other words, the Holy Ghost is doing *His* job (bringing revelations *to* us).

However, President Nelson was talking about *our* responsibility, which is to *receive* the revelations that the Holy Ghost brings to us. In order for us to learn to receive revelation, it must be a given that it is coming to us. President Nelson knows that the Holy Ghost is doing His part. He is encouraging us to do ours. This isn't even a question of worthiness. Without learning how to receive revelation, no matter how worthy we are, we will continue to miss out on important communications that God wants to share with us.

It is very important that you not feel that just because you believe you haven't had any revelations come to you, there must be something wrong with you or your worthiness. If you are doing the things that would keep you worthy, stop worrying. Rather, just do as President Nelson says: Learn how to receive these wonderful revelations from God as delivered to us by the Holy Ghost. And that is what this book will help you do.

"Unto" versus "Into"

To understand the difference between the statements made by Joseph Smith and President Nelson, we should remember what Nephi tells us in 2 Nephi 33:1: "For when a man speaketh by the power of the Holy Ghost the power of the Holy Ghost carrieth it *unto* the hearts of the children of men" (emphasis added). Notice that he says the Holy Ghost carries the message *unto* our hearts. He does not say that He would carry it *into* them. I like to think of it this way: The Holy Ghost does the "heavy lifting." He is the one that takes a message from God and carries it the greatest distance—all the way *unto* our hearts. *The last few inches, however, are totally up to us.* If we want to have it come *into* our hearts, we need to let it in. That's what President Nelson is saying when he tells us that we need to "learn to receive revelation." Of course, first we need to be worthy. And then, we need to learn how to recognize His promptings and distinguish them from all of the "noise" that surrounds us.

A Few Reminders

Personal Worthiness

We won't spend too much time on this subject at all. We know this is important and many books have already been written on the subject. Let's share just two quick quotes:

Elder L. Tom Perry explained that "we do not need man-made rating systems to determine what we should read, what we should watch, what we should listen to, or how we should conduct our lives. **What we do need to do is live worthy of the continued companionship of the Holy Ghost and have the courage to follow the promptings that come into our lives.**"[12]

Elder David A. Bednar told us, "The standard is clear. If something we think, see, hear, or do distances us from the Holy Ghost, then we should stop thinking, seeing, hearing, or doing that thing. If that which is intended to entertain, for example, alienates us from the Holy Spirit, then certainly that type of entertainment is not for us. Because the Spirit cannot abide that which is vulgar, crude, or immodest, then clearly such things are not for us."[13]

The Importance of Prayer

Entire books have been written on the subject of prayer as well. Therefore, I'll limit myself to just one great quote and one important scripture. President Boyd K. Packer said, "Learn to pray. Pray often. Pray in your mind, in your heart. Pray on your knees. **Prayer is your personal key to heaven. The lock is on your side of the veil.**"[14]

After Jesus had first appeared unto the Nephites and then left again, the disciples ministered unto the people. Then, in 3 Nephi 19:9 we read, "**And they did pray for that which they**

---

12. Perry, "Leadeth to Do Good," 70; emphasis added.
13. Bednar, "That We May Always," 30.
14. Packer, "Prayer and Promptings," 46; emphasis added.

most desired; and they desired that the Holy Ghost should be given unto them" (emphasis added). This not only reinforces the importance of praying for the Holy Ghost to be with us, but it also serves as a moving illustration of how important having the Holy Ghost should be to each of us. Note that it was the thing that the disciples "most desired."

Don't Give Up—Too Much Is at Stake

Many of us have felt that the heavens are closed to us. I'm sure that there have been times in your life when you may have felt that your personal prayers have not made it past your bedroom ceiling. On this point, President Russell M. Nelson has said, "To be sure, *there may be times when you feel as though the heavens are closed.* But I promise that as you continue to be obedient, expressing gratitude for every blessing the Lord gives you, and as you patiently honor the Lord's timetable, you will be given the knowledge and understanding you seek. Every blessing the Lord has for you—even miracles—will follow. That is what personal revelation will do for you."[15]

We Will Still Have to Make Some Decisions on Our Own

In our efforts to be led by the Holy Ghost, it is also possible to attempt to *overdo* it. Elder Robert D. Hales said,

> The Holy Ghost provides personal revelation to help us make major life decisions about such things as education, missions, careers, marriage, children, where we will live with our families, and so on. In these matters, Heavenly Father expects us to use our agency, study the situation out in our minds according to gospel principles, and bring a decision to Him in prayer. . . . I remind all of us that the Holy Ghost is not given to control us. **Some of us unwisely seek the Holy Ghost's direction on every minor decision in our lives. This trivializes His sacred role**. The Holy Ghost honors the principle of agency.

15. Nelson, "Revelation for Our Lives," 95–96; emphasis added.

He speaks to our minds and our hearts gently about many matters of consequence.[16]

16. Hales, "Holy Ghost," 105; emphasis added.

CHAPTER 2

How God Talks to Us: The *Bing!*

As we pursue the journey of life,
let us learn the language of the Spirit."

—President Thomas S. Monson[1]

After many of my missionaries shared with me that they felt they had never had a prompting from the Holy Ghost, I knew that I needed to teach them some very important principles about how the Holy Ghost works. I taught them the following.

Principle 1: God Wants to Talk to You

In President Nelson's first general conference as the prophet of the world (April 2018), he made it very clear to us that God *wants* to talk to us. President Nelson said, "One of the things the Spirit has repeatedly impressed upon my mind since my new calling as President of the Church is how willing the Lord is to reveal His mind and will. **The privilege of receiving revelation is one of the greatest gifts of God to His children.**"[2]

It is important to note that President Nelson did *not* say that receiving revelation is one of the greatest gifts of God to His *prophets*. He said that it was one of the greatest gifts of God to His *children*—in other words, to *you and me*! **All of us**!

---

1. Monson, "Spirit Giveth Life," 70.
2. Nelson, "Revelation for Our Lives," 94; emphasis added.

In that same talk, he said, "Does God really *want* to speak to you? Yes!"[3] Then he quoted part of Doctrine and Covenants 121:33: "As well might man stretch forth his puny arm to stop the Missouri river in its decreed course . . . as to hinder the Almighty from pouring down knowledge from heaven upon the heads of the Latter-day Saints." WOW! *Nothing* will stop the Lord from talking to us. If that is the case, the issue isn't on His end; it's always on *our end.*

This concept reminds me of a poem that I first heard when I was a young boy. My mom loved this poem and shared it with her children. The poem "Prayer" is by Carol Lynn Pearson and is found in her book *Beginnings*. It reads as follows:

> This radio set called prayer
> Is designed for remarkably simple repair.
> When the lines fail, there is no doubt
> Which half of the set is out.[4]

Yes, God wants to talk to us. The question is, do we want to listen to Him? The choice, as well as the responsibility, is totally up to us.

Principle 2: God Can Talk to You Any Way He Wants

Too often, possibly because of what the Lord told Oliver Cowdery in Doctrine and Covenants 9:6–9, we have fallen into the trap of believing that in order for us to get a prompting from God, we need to feel a strong and intense "burning in the bosom." That is not always the case. In those verses, He was giving specific direction to Oliver regarding how to translate. While the counsel is good for all of us when we have a decision to make, the Lord has made it clear in other scriptures that He may talk to us in different ways.

We know that God is capable of doing whatever He wants when He chooses to communicate with us. He has shown that He can appear to people, as He did with Moses, Joseph Smith, and others. We have also seen many examples in the scriptures where He has chosen

---

3. Nelson, "Revelation for Our Lives," 95.
4. Pearson, *Beginnings*, 39.

to send a heavenly messenger—an angel—to carry His message to an individual. We remember the angel that appeared to Alma the Younger, an angel that appeared unto Mary, and other similar great manifestations. Further, we have heard of numerous instances where He has chosen to communicate to some people in dreams or with a physical voice, giving people an urgent message such as warning them of imminent danger. There should be no doubt of God's abilities. He can communicate with His children in any way He chooses.

Principle 3: "By Small and Simple Means"

While we can't question the fact that God can communicate with us in any form He chooses, we are mistaken when we believe that when He chooses to communicate with us, it must be—or even will likely be—in one of the above-mentioned, marvelous manifestations.

As a matter of fact, most often, God will *not* communicate with us in any of those ways. It is simply not the way that He typically communicates with His children on earth. In fact, the reason that we hear of those wonderful stories of amazing appearances by God, angels, dreams, and voices in the scriptures is *precisely because they are so unique.*

We should remember what the Book of Mormon prophet Alma taught his son Helaman: "Now ye may suppose that this is foolishness in me; but behold I say unto you, that **by small and simple things are great things brought to pass**; and small means in many instances doth confound the wise. And the Lord God doth work by means to bring about his great and eternal purposes; and **by very small means the Lord doth confound the wise and bringeth about the salvation of many souls**" (Alma 37:6-7; emphasis added).

God is perfect in all that He does. So it only makes sense that He would also be "perfectly efficient" in how He chooses to talk to His children on earth. Why would He appear to us when a prompting—or "whispering"—from the Holy Ghost will suffice? Additionally, we know that we are to learn to live by faith. If God appeared to us and told us how to live, we would not need to use our faith. So, it is vital that we learn to recognize and understand the promptings from the Holy Ghost—and act on them as soon as they come to us—because *that* is how God will almost always communicate with us here on earth. That is, in fact, one of the most important roles of the Holy Ghost. Why would God choose to bypass the Holy Ghost in communicating to us when that is one of the main duties of the Holy Ghost?

God Speaks to Us through the Holy Ghost

Yes, God does still talk to us. And yes, He does so through the Holy Ghost. Elder LeGrand Richards was very direct and clear about how we get revelation from God when he wrote in his monumental book, *A Marvelous Work and a Wonder*, "It must . . . be understood that the Holy Ghost is the medium through whom God and his Son, Jesus Christ, communicate with men [and women] upon the earth."[5]

Three Important Facts

If God will almost always talk to us through the Holy Ghost, then we need to better understand how the Holy Ghost will usually talk to us. I told my missionaries that to better understand this, they first needed to recognize three important facts:

FACT 1: The Holy Ghost is a spirit.
FACT 2: Each of us also has a spirit.
FACT 3: When the Holy Ghost talks to us, it is one spirit (the Holy Ghost) talking to another spirit (our spirit).

These facts seem straightforward and easy to understand, right? The problem is that we have lived in these earthly tabernacles of ours for so long that we have forgotten—and as a result, no longer relate to—how spiritual beings communicate with each other. Prior to coming to earth, it was easy. We didn't even have to think about it. Communication between spirits was natural. It just happened. However, after being in these mortal bodies for however many years we have lived on earth, we are now accustomed to communicating only in a physical way. Therefore, in order to understand how the

5. Richards, *Marvelous Work*, 119.

Holy Ghost talks to us, we need to understand this spiritual communication from our very physical vantage point.

It's as simple as this: When the Holy Ghost talks to people in physical bodies, that prompting—or a "whispering," as it has often been called, since it is so gentle and quiet—will most often seem to us to be just a good idea that pops into our head, out of the blue. I like to call it a *Bing!* moment. All of a sudden, we will have a positive thought that pops into our head (*Bing!*). Or, at least, that's what it will seem like to us as physical beings. But, in reality, it wasn't our own thought at all. It was the Holy Ghost (a spirit) talking to another spirit (our spirit). It's as simple as that. And this has happened to each of us more often than we can count.

Of course, as I have stated earlier, we know that God could appear to us or send an angel to talk to us, but it is usually by "small and simple means" that He deals with us. Why would He appear to us when He can accomplish the same thing by sending us a prompting to our minds—a *Bing!*—from the Holy Ghost, communicating to us in a "small and simple" way?

Bings! Are from God

In order to better illustrate this point of how the Holy Ghost talks to us, let me give you an example that has probably happened to each of us at one time or another: You are watching a TV show. You could be doing anything (gardening, playing video games, ironing, on Pinterest or TikTok, and so on), but in this example, let's say you're watching a TV show. All of a sudden—*Bing!*—a thought pops into your head that you should call your friend that you haven't seen in ten years and haven't even thought about in five years. But, all of a sudden, out of the blue—in the middle of this television show—you get this thought that you should call her. What happens next?

Stop Taking Credit for the Holy Ghost's Promptings

Unfortunately, when this thought comes to you in the middle of the television show, you think it's your own thought or idea that has popped into your head. You don't recognize it as being from the Holy

Ghost because you didn't hear a voice speaking to you or feel a burning in your bosom. You just had a thought pop into your head—a *Bing!* Because you believe that it was merely your own thought, you don't worry too much about it. You say to yourself, "Hmm. That's a good idea. I *will* call her. But right now, I'm into this TV show and I want to see how it ends. I'll call her after the show is over."

Then, after the TV show ends, what happens? That's right—you forget all about that *Bing!* and you don't remember to call her. Later on (perhaps a day or two later), you remember that you had that idea to call her. But you still end up not calling—and you don't even feel bad about not having done so—because, after all, it was just your own insignificant thought, right?

Wrong! Let's think about this for a second. If you haven't seen this person in ten years, nor even thought about her in five years, do you *really* believe that you—*on your own*—would have thought to call her right in the middle of a TV show that has nothing to do with her? Of course not! Don't be silly. There was no reason for you to think about her on your own like that. You only had that *Bing!* because the Holy Ghost knew that she needed to hear from you *right at that moment.* So the Holy Ghost (a spirit) talked to your spirit, and that is why—and how—that positive thought just popped into your head (*Bing!*) in the middle of your TV show. Of course, had you known that it was a prompting from the Holy Ghost, you would have immediately stopped what you were doing and made the phone call to her.

The problem is that since we too often make the mistake of taking credit for the whisperings of the Spirit by believing they are our own thoughts, we make the bigger mistake of *not acting* on those promptings. We need to stop taking credit for communications from a member of the Godhead. As we change the way we view these *Bing!* moments and learn to accept them as promptings from the Holy Ghost, we will begin to play an important role in many miracles—and be the answer to many prayers—in the lives of others.

Is This Backed Up by Scriptures and Living Prophets?

Since everyone can remember situations like this that have happened in our lives, you may now be thinking, "Could this be true?

Could it really be that those thoughts that have popped into my head throughout my life really were promptings from the Holy Ghost? Is what he is teaching in this book backed up by scriptures or prophets?" Let's see what they say about this subject:

What the Scriptures Say

In Doctrine and Covenants 8:2–3, the Lord says, "Yea, behold, **I will tell you in your mind** and in your heart, **by the Holy Ghost**, which shall come upon you and dwell in your heart. **Now, behold, this is the spirit of revelation**" (emphasis added).

In Doctrine and Covenants 11:13, the Lord adds, "Verily, verily, I say unto you, **I will impart unto you of my Spirit, which shall enlighten your mind**, which shall fill your soul with joy" (emphasis added).

In Doctrine and Covenants 6:15, The Lord says further, "And I did **enlighten thy mind**; and now I tell thee these things that thou mayest know that **thou hast been enlightened by the Spirit of truth**" (emphasis added).

And, finally, In Doctrine and Covenants 6:23, the Lord clearly states, "**Did I not speak peace to your mind concerning the matter? What greater witness can you have than from God?**" (emphasis added).

Even Enos, a Book of Mormon prophet, speaks about how the communications he received from God came to his mind. In Enos 1:10, he says, "And while I was thus struggling in the spirit, behold, the voice of the Lord ***came into my mind***" (emphasis added).

What Our Church Leaders Have Said

In the April 1964 general conference, Elder Marion G. Romney referred to the above-mentioned experience by Enos and said, "This is a very common means of revelation. It comes into one's mind in words and sentences. With this medium of revelation, I am personally well acquainted."[6]

Elder David A. Bednar taught about this in the April 2011 general conference. He spoke of Joseph and Oliver and what they learned

6. Romney, "About Revelation," 124.

about revelation as they worked on the translation of the Book of Mormon: "Over time they increasingly understood **the spirit of revelation typically functions as thoughts and feelings that come into our minds and hearts by the power of the Holy Ghost**."[7]

Elder Boyd K. Packer, in the April 2000 general conference, said: "The voice of the Spirit is a still, small voice—a voice that is felt rather than heard. **It is a spiritual voice that comes into the mind as a thought put into your heart**."[8]

How Can We Tell the Difference between Our Thoughts and a Prompting?

In every zone conference where I taught our missionaries that these positive thoughts, or *Bings!*, are really promptings from God that we need to act on, I would immediately have hands go up. Almost every time, the first question that I would get would go something like this: "President, this sounds great. Thank you for teaching this to us. But how will I be able to tell the difference between a prompting from the Holy Ghost and my own thoughts?" I would then look around and see the faces of many other missionaries nodding in agreement to this question, also wanting to know the answer.

I always responded with the same reply. "Elder (or Sister), that is a great question. I want you to write my answer down so you won't forget it. Are you ready?" At this point, not only the person who asked the question but almost every other missionary was also ready, pen in hand, to write down the answer. Then, I would say, "It doesn't matter! **Just act on it**!" Immediately, I would hear a bunch of groans and some saying, "Of *course* it matters!" However, before they could say anything else, I would say, "Think about it for a second. Let's say that it really was your own idea to call that friend from ten years ago—or to do some other positive thing. It probably wasn't. The odds are much greater that it was the Holy Ghost, but just for the sake of argument, let's say that *this one time,* it really was your idea to do this positive thing instead of it being a prompting from the Holy Ghost. If you act

7. Bednar, "Spirit of Revelation," 88; emphasis added.
8. Packer, "Cloven Tongues," 8; emphasis added.

on that positive thought of yours, do you think that God will be mad at you for having done so? *Of course not!* He will be happy that you are trying to bless the life of one of His children."

Then, after pausing a bit and letting that sink in for a second, I would continue, "However, now that we have thought about how God would feel if that was the case, let's consider how He would feel if the tables were turned. What if the prompting really was from the Holy Ghost—it really was what God wanted you to do—but you thought it was your own thought and didn't act on it? What happens then? I worry that, if you choose *not* to act on a prompting from God, you risk losing God's confidence in you acting on the promptings that He sends you. The next time He needs to bless someone's life, shouldn't He give the prompting to someone who *will* act on it?"

Now, I know that last part may have sounded a bit rough. And I also know that there are no "surprises" to God. Whether we act on a prompting of His or not, He already knows how we will respond. But it is a pattern that we set for ourselves. Just as we know that we learn and grow "line upon line," so it is with our growth in acting on promptings.

In the October 2012 general conference, President Thomas S. Monson said, "My brothers and sisters, the Lord's purposes are often accomplished as we pay heed to the guidance of the Spirit. **I believe that the more we act upon the inspiration and impressions which come to us, the more the Lord will entrust to us His errands**."[9] If the prophet of the Lord believes that the more we act on the impressions, the more the Lord will entrust us with more promptings, doesn't it make sense that the *less* we act on His promptings, the *less* He will want to give promptings to us? I certainly believe so.

Nine Times Out of Ten—Those Are Pretty Good Odds

Finally, in order to help you feel even more comfortable with the idea of following those *Bings!* when you get them, let's refer to what one of the world's experts on revelation had to say regarding this

9. Monson, "Consider the Blessings," 86–87; emphasis added.

topic. Joseph Smith said, "**If you will listen to the first promptings, you will get it right nine times out of ten**."[10] In other words, it is almost *always* the Holy Ghost who is prompting us to do this good thing. And the very few times that it is *not* a prompting from the Holy Ghost, God will still be pleased with us that we are acting on a good thought to help another.

Just Do It!

After helping the missionaries understand that as long as it was a positive thought they really didn't need to worry about whether it was their own thought or a prompting from the Holy Ghost, I introduced a new rule for us to follow in our mission. This "rule" was something that I had heard from my brother-in-law, Joe Johnson. I have great love and respect for President/Dr. Joe. He recently retired and turned his practice as a family physician over to his son. He is a great man of God who is always seeking to serve others. Even though he has physically helped so many people throughout his career, I believe he has healed even more people spiritually because that is his true desire—and his gift! At the time he shared this quote with me, he was serving as the stake president of the Sparks Nevada Stake. However, now he and his wife, JoEllen (my younger sister), serve as mission president and companion of the Michigan Detroit Mission. His quote (and our new mission rule) was as follows: "Any positive thought to say or do something is a **prompting from God until proven otherwise**. *Just act on it*!" I wanted our mission to always assume that every positive thought that came into their minds was of God. I wanted them to just act on the prompting.

Scriptures and a Prophet Support Our "Mission Rule"

This quote from Joe Johnson states in laymen's terms what the Lord has already told us in the scriptures. In Doctrine and Covenants 11:12, the Lord says, "And now, verily, verily, I say unto thee, put your trust in that Spirit which leadeth to do good—yea, to do justly, to walk humbly, to judge righteously; and this is my Spirit." Doesn't that seem

10. Madsen, *Joseph Smith*, 103; emphasis added.

like it is telling us the same thing? The Lord is not even telling you to worry about it being "proven otherwise." He is saying to simply trust that it is from Him. We can rest assured that any positive thought to say or do something is a prompting from God. We just need to commit to act on it immediately.

President Gordon B. Hinckley taught us the same thing in his answer to the question, "How do we recognize the promptings of the Spirit?" First, he read Moroni 7:13, 16–17:

> But behold, that which is of God inviteth and enticeth to do good continually; wherefore, every thing which inviteth and enticeth to do good, and to love God, and to serve Him, is inspired of God. For behold, the Spirit of Christ is given to every man [and woman], that he [or she] may know good from evil; wherefore, I show unto you the way to judge; for every thing which inviteth to do good, and to persuade to believe in Christ, is sent forth by the power and gift of Christ; wherefore ye may know with a perfect knowledge it is of God. But whatsoever thing persuadeth men to do evil, and believe not in Christ, and deny him, and serve not God, then ye may know with a perfect knowledge that it is of the devil; for after this manner doth the devil work, for he persuadeth no man to do good, no, not one; neither do his angels; neither do they who subject themselves unto him.

Then, President Hinckley said:

> That's the test, when all is said and done. Does it persuade one to do good, to rise, to stand tall, to do the right thing, to be kind, to be generous? Then it is of the Spirit of God. . . . If it invites to do good, it is of God. If it inviteth to do evil, it is of the devil. . . . And if you are doing the right thing and if you are living the right way, you will know in your heart what the Spirit is saying to you. You recognize the promptings of the Spirit by the fruits of the Spirit—that which enlighteneth, that which buildeth up, that which is positive and affirmative

> and uplifting and leads us to better thoughts and better words and better deeds is of the Spirit of God.[11]

The *Bing!* Will Often Be a Feeling

Many times you have "felt" that you should do something. I hope this chapter will help you understand that your positive feelings are promptings from the Holy Ghost, and, as a result, you will *immediately* stop what you are doing and act on that feeling.

President Boyd K. Packer taught, "**Revelation comes as words we *feel*** more than ***hear***. Nephi told his wayward brothers, who were visited by an angel, '**Ye were past *feeling*, that ye could not *feel*** his words' [1 Nephi 17:45]."[12]

You notice that Nephi does not say, "Ye could not *hear* his words," but rather, "Ye could not *feel* his words." That is not a natural way to speak about how we receive physical words when another person speaks to us. Yet it fits perfectly when talking about the voice of the Spirit because He is typically a voice that we can *feel* rather than *hear*.

Elder Ronald A. Rasband taught this same principle. In his April 2017 general conference address he said, "**My experience has been that the Spirit most often communicates as a feeling. You feel it in words that are familiar to you, that make sense to you, that prompt you.**"[13]

Finally, we will summarize this point with one more message from Elder Boyd K. Packer on the subject:

> **These delicate, refined spiritual communications are not seen with our eyes, nor heard with our ears. And even though it is described as a voice, it is a voice that one feels more than one hears. . . .**
>
> **The Spirit does not get our attention by shouting or shaking us with a heavy hand. Rather it whispers. It caresses so gently that if we are preoccupied we may not**

---

11. Hinckley, *Teachings*, 260–61.
12. Packer, 60; emphasis added.
13. Rasband, "Holy Spirit Guide," 94; emphasis added.

> **feel it at all**. . . . Occasionally it will press just firmly enough for us to pay heed. But **most of the time, if we do not heed the gentle feeling, the Spirit will withdraw and wait until we come seeking and listening and say in our manner and expression, like Samuel of ancient times, "Speak [Lord], for thy servant heareth"** (1 Sam. 3:10).[14]

You've Never Heard a Voice or Seen an Angel? So What!

While I love reading about the remarkable visions and hearing of other faith-promoting experiences where people have heard voices and the like, I worry that the sharing of these stories, in some cases, has done more harm than good. Some people have felt that these are the only ways that the Holy Ghost communicates, and because this hasn't happened to them, they feel that there is something wrong with them, even though they have tried to live the best life that they possibly could live. Others are still anxiously waiting for similar experiences to occur in their lives—even though the Lord has been trying to communicate to them with the *Bings!*—or the promptings—from the Holy Ghost and they keep failing to understand that those messages are from God.

One of my purposes in writing this book is to help all of us who have felt or are currently feeling this way to *quit beating ourselves up!* While these stories are great, as I mentioned earlier, the reason they are so exciting to hear about is that they are so far out of the norm. It is simply *not* how God will usually communicate with His children here on earth.

Elder David A. Bednar taught this principle much better than I just did when he said,

> **We as members of the Church tend to emphasize marvelous and dramatic spiritual manifestations so much that we may fail to appreciate and may even overlook the customary pattern by which the Holy Ghost accomplishes His work.** The very 'simpleness of the way' (1 Nephi 17:41) of receiving

---

14. Packer, "Candle of the Lord," 52–53; emphasis added.

> small and incremental spiritual impressions that over time and in totality constitute a desired answer or the direction we need may cause us to look 'beyond the mark' (Jacob 4:14). **I have talked with many individuals who question the strength of their personal testimony and underestimate their spiritual capacity because they do not receive frequent, miraculous, or strong impressions**. Perhaps as we consider the experiences of Joseph in the Sacred Grove, of Saul on the road to Damascus, and of Alma the Younger, we come to believe something is wrong with or lacking in us if we fall short in our lives of these well-known and spiritually striking examples. **If you have had similar thoughts or doubts, please know that you are quite normal. Just keep pressing forward obediently and with faith in the Savior. As you do so, you 'cannot go amiss'** (Doctrine and Covenants 80:3).[15]

President Spencer W. Kimball spoke regarding this challenge in the Church as well. In *Teachings of Spencer W. Kimball* (and referred to by Elder Boyd K. Packer in his October 1994 general conference talk), he told us that we should not seek for spectacular experiences. He spoke of the many who "have no ear for spiritual messages . . . when they come in common dress. . . . **Expecting the spectacular, one may not be fully alerted to the constant flow of revealed communication.**"[16]

Did you notice how he referred to God's communication to us as being a "constant flow"? Wow! We are missing out on so much. And this is all because we are not looking for the small and simple ways that He almost always chooses to talk to us.

The Prophet Teaches Us How to Get Personal Revelation

Who better to teach us about how to receive revelation than a living prophet of God? Let's review what President Russell M. Nelson has taught us on this subject. In the April 2018 general conference, he gave a talk entitled "Revelation for the Church, Revelation for Our

15. Bednar, "Spirit of Revelation," 88–89; emphasis added.
16. Kimball, *Teachings*, 457; emphasis added.

Lives." In this landmark address, he taught us, step by step, what we need to do to get personal revelation: "Pray in the name of Jesus Christ about your concerns, your fears, your weaknesses—yes, the very longings of your heart. And then listen! **Write the thoughts that come to your mind. Record your feelings and follow through with actions that you are prompted to take. As you repeat this process day after day, month after month, year after year, you will 'grow into the principle of revelation.'"**[17]

In this message, our prophet told us that *the thoughts that come into our minds (these Bings!) are promptings from God (through the Holy Ghost).* This is an extremely important principle for us to understand and internalize. He made a point to tell us to write those thoughts down and to follow through with the actions we are prompted to take. President Nelson doesn't want us to be fooled any further into thinking that these thoughts are our own thoughts.

Another important principle that President Nelson taught us in that talk was that as we act on the promptings of the Holy Ghost, we will get better and better at it. President Nelson pointed out that "as you repeat this process day after day, month after month, year after year, you will **'grow into the principle of revelation**.'"[18]

Tuning Our Celestial Radios

I also taught my missionaries this same principle and referred to it as tuning in their "celestial radios." I used the analogy of the old radios of yesteryear. Do you remember how, when we wanted to listen to a certain station, we had to grab the knob and tune it in carefully to get the best possible reception of that station? In my opinion, that is exactly what we are doing every time we act on a prompting from the Holy Ghost. Each time we act on a prompting, we are getting more and more in tune with the Spirit—so that the next time, it will be easier still to recognize the prompting. However, every time we get a prompting and we do *not* act on it, we are tuning ourselves *away* from "God's station." And, the next time, it will be more difficult to

---

17. Nelson, "Revelation for Our Lives," 95; emphasis added.
18. Nelson, 95; emphasis added.

recognize the prompting when it comes. To me, besides living worthily, this is an extremely important part of how we "grow into the principle of revelation."

I promised my missionaries that, over time, as they acted on their promptings, they would begin to notice it becoming easier and easier to recognize those promptings each time in the future ("growing into the spirit of revelation"). Their promptings would begin to seem louder and louder (and clearer) each time. Thus, they would become easier to recognize. In reality, it wouldn't be because the promptings would be getting louder. Rather, it would be because they themselves are becoming much more "in tune" to the Spirit. I had a number of missionaries who shared with me—as they began to test this out—that they were quickly seeing differences and were loving it.

The results of "tuning in our celestial radios" were also taught to us by President Henry B. Eyring. Speaking of promptings, he said, **"Whatever it is, do it. When you demonstrate your willingness to obey, the Spirit will send you more impressions of what God would have you do for Him. As you obey, the impressions from the Spirit will come more frequently, becoming closer and closer to constant companionship. Your power to choose the right will increase.**"[19]

Elder Bednar also spoke very clearly on this topic:

> We are prompted by the Holy Ghost every day to do ordinary and simple things. . . . **To the degree that we heed these simple promptings, then our capacity to recognize and respond to the Holy Ghost is increased. To the degree that we do not heed these simple promptings, then our capacity to recognize and respond to the Holy Ghost is decreased. We are either progressing or regressing in our ability to recognize and respond to the Holy Ghost. There is no neutral ground; there is no standing still.**
>
> The law of the harvest is real; we cannot gather crops in the fall which we did not properly plant and cultivate during the spring and summer. **And we cannot realistically expect**

---

19. Eyring, "As Your Companion," 105; emphasis added.

> **to recognize "*big*" promptings if we consistently fail to heed the "*small*" ones. The Lord's pattern is to teach us "*. . . line upon line, precept upon precept, here a little and there a little . . .*" (2 Nephi 28:30).**[20]

He made it very clear. We are, in fact, either tuning ourselves in better and better to the Spirit or tuning ourselves out more and more. And it is very important to remember that *we* are the ones who have control of our "radio dial."

Elder Richard G. Scott added, "As you gain experience and success in being guided by the Spirit, your confidence in the impressions you feel can become more certain than your dependence on what you see or hear."[21]

How It Works for a Prophet of God

As you can imagine, a prophet of God has his "celestial radio" dialed in perfectly well. Sister Wendy Nelson learned this after her husband became the prophet. In an article about her personal witness of her husband's prophetic calling, we read the following: "After marrying President Nelson in 2006, Sister Nelson had, on numerous occasions, witnessed him receive revelation from the Lord during the night, especially as general conference approached. But after he was ordained as the Lord's prophet, the revelation came with frequency and intensity."

The story continues:

> For example, early one Saturday morning, Sister Nelson awoke and knew she was to get out of bed. She was not done sleeping, but she could feel the prompting to "move out of bed now."
>
> "So, I went downstairs and did some family history research and then puttered with some other things," she recalled. "Two hours later, my husband emerged from our bedroom and said,

20. Bednar, "Receiving, Recognizing, and Responding"; emphasis added.
21. Scott, "To Acquire Spiritual Guidance," 7.

> 'Wendy, you won't believe what has been happening for two hours. The Lord has given me detailed instruction about a process I am to follow.' "
>
> Other times the Lord has prompted Sister Nelson to stay close to her husband when he is receiving instruction. "My husband will say during the night, 'OK, dear, it is happening.' I remain quiet, and then soon he is sitting up on the side of the bed writing."[22]

What a great article about our remarkable prophet. Can you imagine? He is so "in tune" that he needs to keep a notepad and pen on the nightstand next to his bed in order to be ready at any time—day or night—for the Lord to instruct him. And, as we have read, many times the Lord chooses to talk to him during the middle of the night.

God Has Called Us to Be Angels in Disguise

While God will occasionally give us promptings that will be for our benefit, much more frequently, He will prompt us (with *Bings!* from the Holy Ghost) to come to the aid of others. Perhaps it will help your immediate family members or friends. It could also benefit a work associate or classmate—or even a complete stranger. With these promptings, we are in essence being called by God to be "angels" in the lives of other people. Since God is using us instead of angels on the other side of the veil, we can think of ourselves as "angels in disguise." It is exciting to think about our ability to *literally* serve as angels in the lives of others.

I recall two outstanding general conference talks on this subject. They are both beautiful talks, and I highly recommend giving them another read or listen. I am sharing here only one quote from each of them. The first was given by Elder Jeffrey R. Holland in October 2008 and is entitled "The Ministry of Angels." In that talk, Elder Holland said, "My beloved brothers and sisters, I testify of angels, both the heavenly and the mortal kind. In doing so I am testifying that God

---

22. Weaver, "Sister Wendy Nelson Shares."

never leaves us alone, never leaves us unaided in the challenges that we face."[23]

The second talk, entitled "I Believe in Angels," was given by Elder Carlos A. Godoy in October 2020. He said, "The Lord is aware of the challenges they face, and He is looking for angels willing to help. The Lord is always looking for willing volunteers to be angels in others' lives. Brothers and sisters, would you be willing to be an instrument in the Lord's hands? Would you be willing to be one of these angels? To be an emissary, sent from God, from this side of the veil, for someone He is worried about? He needs you. They need you."[24]

The messages from Elder Holland and Elder Godoy are clear and strong. Let's decide today to be angels in the lives of others and act on the many promptings—the *Bings!*—that God is sending our way—like the *Bing!* to call the friend we hadn't seen in ten years while we were watching TV. It will take courage, but courage is needed by any good soldier. And we are deciding to become soldiers in God's army to save the lives of those around us—physically and spiritually. We truly are in a war with the adversary for the souls of God's children. These are exciting—and very important—times.

Don't Overlook the Added Benefit to Us Individually

I am sure many of you can remember times in your life when you went to a service project or to make a home teaching or visiting teaching visit—back when we had home teachers and visiting teachers—even though you had absolutely no desire to do so. Yet, in the process of fulfilling that duty, the Spirit filled your soul and you came back from having done so feeling much better than when you left and were almost embarrassed with how you felt before you left to go serve. Why do you think that happened? You see, the Lord changes who we are as we serve other people. He helps us become better people. We are, in fact, without even knowing it, "coming unto Christ" as we serve His brothers and sisters. Why? Because of the work we are in. The hint is found in what we are told in Mosiah 2:17: "And behold,

23. Holland, 31.
24. Godoy, 87.

I tell you these things that ye may learn wisdom; that ye may learn that when ye are in the service of your fellow beings ye are only in the service of your God."

Elder Dieter F. Uchtdorf shared yet another personal blessing from God that will come to us as we obey and act on the promptings of the Holy Ghost: "Let us listen to and ***obey the promptings of the Holy Spirit.*** **As we do so, Heavenly Father will reveal to us things we never knew about ourselves.** He will illuminate the path ahead and open our eyes **to see our unknown and perhaps unimagined talents.**"[25]

It is not my intent to inspire us to become angels in the lives of others by pointing out "selfish" reasons to serve. Rather, I just want to remind each of us that, like everything else in God's wonderful plan for His children, those who serve are oftentimes blessed by God just as much—and sometimes even more, but in different ways—than those we are serving.

Examples of *Bing!* Moments—Revelation Comes to All of Us

Now that we have spoken of how the Holy Ghost will most often talk to us, let's consider just a few short stories that provide some examples of his *Bings!* in our daily lives:

Finding the Sacrament in Australia

In the October 2015 general conference, President Henry B. Eyring shared a story about his father that had happened years earlier when his father's work took him to Australia:

> He was alone on a Sunday, and he wanted to take the sacrament. He could find no information about [Church of Jesus Christ of Latter-day Saint] meetings. So he started walking. He prayed at each intersection to know which way to turn. After walking and making turns for an hour, he stopped to pray again. He felt an impression to turn down a particular

25. Uchtdorf, "Of Regrets and Resolutions," 23; emphasis added.

> street. Soon he began to hear singing coming from the ground floor of an apartment building close by. He looked in at the window and saw a few people seated near a table covered with a white cloth and sacrament trays. Now, that may not seem like much to you, but it was something wonderful to him.[26]

President Eyring said his father prayed at each intersection to know which way to turn. Did he hear a voice? No. He felt "impressions" (*Bings!*) and he followed each one. It may seem small to you, but just think of the miracles that took place to guide him all the way to the one and only place he wanted to find.

Sticking His Foot in the Door

In the April 2017 general conference, Elder Ronald A. Rasband shared a great story from his time as a young missionary in Scotch Plains, New Jersey, that portrayed a wonderful example of the positive results that can come from following a prompting from the Holy Ghost (a *Bing!*). He said:

> One hot July morning my companion and I felt prompted to look up a Temple Square referral. We knocked on the door of the Elwood Schaffer home. Mrs. Schaffer politely turned us away.
>
> As she began to shut the door, I felt to do something I had never done before and have never done since! I stuck my foot in the door, and I asked, "Is there anyone else who might be interested in our message?" Her 16-year-old daughter, Marti, did have an interest and had fervently prayed for guidance just the day before. Marti met with us, and in time her mother participated in the discussions. Both of them joined the Church.
>
> Resulting from Marti's baptism, 136 people, including many of her own family, have been baptized and made gospel covenants. How grateful I am that I listened to the Spirit and stuck my foot in the door on that hot July day.[27]

---

26. Eyring, "As Your Companion," 105–6.
27. Rasband, "Holy Spirit Guide," 94.

Did you notice how, in Elder Rasband's story, he was prompted twice? His first *Bing!* was when he felt prompted to look up the referral that led them to that home. His second *Bing!* came when the woman was shutting the door on him. The Lord did not want that to happen, so Elder Rasband had a strange thought—a prompting to do something that he had "never done before and [has] never done since." He was prompted to stick his foot in the door and ask if anyone else might be interested in their message. How glad he must have been that he acted on the prompting—that *Bing!*—even though, logically, it may not have seemed as the "right thing" to do at the time. Left to his own judgment, I'm sure that this was something that he would not have done on his own. However, the Holy Ghost knew better.

Follow the Positive Thought and Good Things Will Happen

This next story is one very similar to those that have surely happened to many missionaries around the world. And perhaps they didn't even recognize that it was the Holy Ghost talking to them at the time. This one happened to two great missionaries who served with us in the Brazil São Paulo Interlagos Mission.

Elder Paiva and Elder Richins were seeking out less-active members to minister to on a cold rainy night in São Paulo, Brazil. They were soaked and chilled to the bone, and after not having much success, they knew they wouldn't be cheating the Lord to go home now, because it was getting close to the time to be heading home anyway. They were just about to give up for the night when Elder Paiva turned to Elder Richins and said, "I feel that we should try one more house on our list before we go home." They just happened to be on the right street for that name on the list. They clapped at the gate of the house, as is the custom in Brazil. Elder Richins told me later that he assumed nobody would even answer the door with the rain pounding down as it was. Someone did answer the door, and she let the two soaked missionaries in. They shared a message and returned many times after that, with other messages. She returned to full activity in the Church. Her daughter served a mission. Her boyfriend was baptized, and after the two missionaries returned home from their missions, she and that former boyfriend—now her husband—were sealed in the São Paulo

Brazil Temple. Later, she shared with Elder Richins why she let them in that night.

She had been longing to return to activity in the Church but didn't know how to do it. She got on her knees and said a prayer, asking God to give her the strength she needed to return to church. She said that right after she got up from her prayer, the missionaries clapped at her door. Doesn't this give you a better understanding as to why Elder Paiva felt they should try "one more house"? He was receiving a *Bing!*—a prompting from the Holy Ghost. She also told Elder Richins that he and his companion looked an awful lot like the two missionaries who had baptized her years previously, who also showed up at her door on a cold and rainy night.

Any Positive Thought Means *Any* Positive Thought

Elder Jacob Moos was another wonderful, faithful missionary who served with us in the Brazil São Paulo Interlagos Mission. Like many missionaries when they first arrive on the mission, he shared with me that he was experiencing some real challenges with following the Spirit. This was not due to any type of disobedience but simply a challenge in being able to *recognize the promptings* of the Spirit. He would almost always dismiss thoughts that would come to him as being his own thoughts and would not act on them. Then, one day, we had an interview where I challenged him to act on *any and all positive thoughts that came to him, without any question.* If it wasn't a thought to do something wrong, I told him that he needed to simply act on it.

Soon after that interview, he was crossing a street and saw a crudely made handwritten sign for an "unofficial" street. On the sign, he saw that someone had given a Japanese name for that particular "street." Immediately a thought popped into his head about how he had always wanted to teach someone who was Japanese. Before he could even start in that direction, however, he had another thought that popped into his head. He assumed that this second thought was his own thought. (We will talk about these other thoughts in an upcoming chapter.) The second thought was this: "What a foolish reason to go down this street just because I've always wanted to teach a Japanese person."

However, Elder Moos remembered that he had promised his mission president that he would act on *any* non-negative thought. So, away he went to knock on doors on this street. He later reported to me that on that street alone, they found not one—not two—but *three* amazing (although stubborn) families. And they later found out that two of those families had just finished praying to God, asking for help in their lives.

Within a few short weeks, Elder Moos and his companion baptized two of the families. After helping the father and mother of the third family get legally married, they baptized them, as well. Elder Moos learned a great lesson about the importance of acting on those positive thoughts that he had previously dismissed as being his own thoughts. It was obvious to him that God, indeed, wanted him and his companion to go down that "unofficial" street with a Japanese name on that very night.

Sometimes, the *Bings!* May Be Physical

Sometimes, in order to answer the prayer of another, the Lord has to do more than give us a little thought or a spiritual "nudge" to have us be the answer to someone's prayer. Here is an example of how God sometimes has to make the *Bing!* be a little bit stronger.

One day, a number of years ago, my oldest brother, Mike, was driving down the highway on a very hot California summer day. He didn't have air conditioning in his car, so he had his windows down as he was driving. All of a sudden, a big gust of wind caught the open map that was on his dashboard. It flew up and stuck right on his face as he was driving. (Note: For you younger readers, a number of years ago, maps were printed on very large pieces of paper that were folded intricately. We didn't have the amazingly simple ones we have on our phones now. I know, you are thinking that we had it pretty rough, right?)

Mike was startled, and as he reached for the map, he accidentally hit the gear shift and knocked the car out of gear and into neutral. His car drifted over toward the median of the highway and came to a stop right behind another car that was also in the median. He looked at the car ahead of him and saw a woman in the driver's seat. After all of the "physical help" that the Spirit had already made happen, Mike told me that, all of a sudden, he had a *Bing!* moment. He felt strongly that the female driver in that car needed help.

When Mike shared this story with me, he said that he told the Lord, "Okay, you don't have to hit me over the head with a baseball bat."

Then he thought about what had just happened. He felt another thought pop into his head that said, "Yes, I do."

Then Mike confessed, "Okay, maybe you do."

Mike got out of his car and walked up to the driver's window of the other car. Even though it was a blazing hot summer day, that poor woman had all of the car windows rolled up. He figured that she must have been very afraid for her safety. He could see that her head was bowed, as if in prayer.

Mike tapped on her window. She cracked it just enough to communicate, and Mike asked her if she needed any help. She said that she had run out of gas. Mike said that he would go get her some gas and be right back. He got back into his car and drove to the next exit. He found a gas station and bought a gallon of gas and took it back to her car and emptied it into her gas tank. She immediately started her car and was on her way, no doubt with a newfound testimony that God answers personal prayers.

I hope that the principles taught in this chapter—together with the stories about applying those principles in our lives—have motivated you to re-evaluate the positive thoughts that have popped into your head in the past. The Lord has a lot of His children to bless, and the Holy Ghost is very busy communicating those messages to us. It is simply a matter of our need to recognize, accept, and act on those promptings—those *Bing!* moments—when they come to us.

SECTION TWO

The Second *Bing!*

CHAPTER 3

Satan Is Also a Spirit

"Nothing is a greater injury to the children of men than to be under the influence of a false spirit when they think they have the Spirit of God."

—Joseph Smith[1]

As we begin to understand how the Holy Ghost speaks to us—how spirits communicate with each other—we need to recognize another very important fact: The adversary is also a spirit. And, as a spirit, he talks to us in the same manner that the Holy Ghost speaks to us. Oftentimes, his promptings will come to us as a simple thought that has popped into our head, just like the *Bings!* we have already spoken of. He does this constantly in our lives. Far too often, people don't see his promptings for what they are—messages from the enemy of our souls. Instead, just as we have done with the promptings of the Holy Ghost, we most often believe that these promptings from him are just our own thoughts that have popped into our heads. Or, worse still (although far less frequent), as the quote from Joseph Smith pointed out at the beginning of this chapter, at times we may actually believe that one of his promptings was a prompting from the Holy Ghost.

---

1. Smith, Joseph, *Teachings of the Prophet*, 211.

The Adversary and His Goals

The First Presidency of the Church of Jesus Christ of Latter-day Saints spoke directly about the adversary in one of their messages: "He is working under such perfect disguise that **many do not recognize either him or his methods**. There is no crime he would not commit, no debauchery he would not set up, no plague he would not send, no heart he would not break, no life he would not take, no soul he would not destroy. He comes as a thief in the night; **he is a wolf in sheep's clothing**."[2]

In Doctrine & Covenants 10:27, we read: "And thus he goeth up and down, to and fro in the earth, seeking to destroy the souls of men." That is the goal of the adversary—"***to destroy the souls of men***"! In fact, Elder Marion G. Romney was even more direct when he told the world in a general conference address, "**Satan is evil: totally and always**. He ever seeks to defeat the gospel plan and 'destroy the souls of men' (Doctrine and Covenants 10:27)."[3]

For those who doubt that the adversary can talk to us in the same way that the Holy Ghost can, it is my sincere hope that you will reconsider as you read further. He absolutely *can* and *does* talk to us in this way. All spirits are governed by the same rules. Therefore, it makes sense that his communication to us would be done in the same way. It is one spirit (his spirit—or the spirit of one of his servants) talking to our spirit. And we will "hear" his communications in the same way that we "hear" promptings from the Holy Ghost. They will appear to be simply a thought that pops into our head and will seem just like another *Bing!* And, just as it is with promptings from the Holy Ghost, they will usually come to us as more of a feeling or a thought than something we actually hear.

Because of this fact, not only is it imperative that we continually become much better at recognizing the voice of the Spirit, but we must also become experts at recognizing the voice of the adversary so that we can kick his promptings out of our mind and heart as soon as they arrive and *never* act on them.

---

2. Clark, *Messages*, 6:179; emphasis added.
3. Romney, "Great Deceiver," 36; emphasis added.

Getting People to Believe There Is No Devil

One of Satan's favorite tricks is to convince mankind that he doesn't even exist. He tries to get people to believe that they are too educated to believe in a devil. Nephi tells us, "And behold, others he flattereth away, and telleth them there is no hell; and he saith unto them: I am no devil, for there is none—and thus he **whispereth in their ears**, until he grasps them with his awful chains, from whence there is no deliverance" (2 Nephi 28:22; emphasis added).

Elder Boyd K. Packer Warns of the Adversary's Tricks

Elder Boyd K. Packer spoke and taught frequently about the Holy Ghost. However, in a number of his talks, he has given us some great counsel regarding the adversary as well. Let's look at some of his teachings on the subject:

In his April 2000 general conference address, he said, "And soon we learn that **the tempter—the adversary—uses those same channels of the mind and heart to inspire us to evil, to laziness, to contention, even to acts of darkness. He can take over our thoughts** and lead us to mischief. But each of us has agency; ever and always light presides over darkness."[4]

Additionally, in his October 1994 general conference address, Elder Packer warned, "**There can be counterfeit revelations, promptings from the devil**, temptations! As long as you live, in one way or another the adversary will try to lead you astray."[5]

Warnings from Other Prophets of the Reality of Satan

It makes sense that, since Lucifer and his followers didn't come to earth to gain bodies, they did not have to pass through the veil of forgetfulness that we all did in order to be tested here on earth. In fact, they would *need* to remember the premortal world. If Satan and his followers passed through the veil as we did, they wouldn't know that they needed to fight against God and His plan. As we read the conversations that Satan had in the Garden of Eden with Adam and Eve,

---

4. Packer, "Cloven Tongues," 9; emphasis added.
5. Packer, "Personal Revelation," 61; emphasis added.

it also indicates that he did not pass through the veil. By remembering all that went on before we came to earth, he is much more focused on his goal to overthrow God's plan.

This means that Satan and his followers know each of our individual strengths and weaknesses from fighting against us and living with us before they were sent away from God's presence. On top of that, they have had many years of experience—watching us on this earth—learning our weaknesses and strengths here.

President Spencer W. Kimball said, "Lucifer and his followers know the habits, weaknesses, and vulnerable spots of everyone and take advantage of them to lead us to spiritual destruction."[6]

Joseph F. Smith taught us that "by every possible means he seeks to darken the minds of men, and then **offers them falsehood and deception in the guise of truth**. Satan is a skillful imitator, and as genuine gospel truth is given the world in ever-increasing abundance, so **he spreads the counterfeit coin of false doctrine**. . . . [As] 'the father of lies' he has . . . become, through the ages of practice in his nefarious work, [so adept] that were it possible he would deceive the very elect."[7] President Smith is warning us that Satan will try to copy (and slightly tweak) things that are from God so that what we hear from him—and from those that follow him—will "sound right" to us. **We *must* be extremely careful and always be on our guard.**

President Joseph Fielding Smith said that Satan can spread his message "in the person of a friend or a relative in whom we have confidence. **He has power to place thoughts in our minds and to whisper to us in unspoken impressions** to entice us to satisfy our appetites or desires and in various ways he plays upon our weaknesses and desires."[8]

The Lord Himself warned the Nephites about Satan when he appeared unto them: "Behold, verily, verily, I say unto you, ye must watch and pray always lest ye enter into temptation; for Satan desireth to have you, that he may sift you as wheat" (3 Nephi 18:18). He

---

6. Kimball, Miracle of Forgiveness, 218–19.
7. Smith, Joseph F., *Gospel Doctrine*, 376; emphasis added.
8. Smith, Joseph Fielding, *Answers to Gospel Questions*, 3:81; emphasis added.

warned us more recently, as well. In Doctrine and Covenants 50:2–3, He said (after many of the elders of the Church had been fooled by false spirits), "Behold, verily I say unto you, that there are many spirits which are false spirits, which have gone forth in the earth, deceiving the world. And also, Satan hath sought to deceive you, that he might overthrow you."

Worse still, we may even get false revelations from the adversary. David Whitmer said that the Prophet Joseph Smith taught that "some revelations are of God: some revelations are of man: and *some revelations are of the devil.*"[9]

Brigham Young also talked about Satan and his followers—and just how hard they are working against us at all times:

> I know very well that, whether we are active or not, **the invisible spirits are active**. And every person who desires and strives to be a Saint is closely watched by fallen spirits that came here when Lucifer fell, and by the spirits of wicked persons who have been here in tabernacles and departed from them, but who are still under the control of the prince of the power of the air. **Those spirits are never idle; they are watching every person who wishes to do right, and are *continually prompting them to do wrong*. This makes it necessary for us to be continually on guard**—makes this probation a continual warfare. We do not expect to be idle. **The individual that obtains a celestial kingdom will never be idle in the flesh. It is a spiritual warfare.**[10]

What a strong and important message! It is one of the reasons that I have felt so compelled to write this book and help "pull back the curtain" regarding what Satan is doing to us on a daily basis. I know this and have experienced it myself. For years, even as a good member of the Church who had been trying to do the right things and live worthily my whole life, I was still falling for the tricks of the adversary on a regular basis. And the whole reason I was falling for his tricks

9. Roberts, *Comprehensive History*, 1:163; emphasis added.
10. Young, *Journal of Discourses*, 7:239; emphasis added.

was that I didn't recognize that his promptings really were promptings from him. I usually thought they were my own thoughts. And, many times, they made a lot of sense. They were logical thoughts.

Can Satan Read Our Thoughts?

This is an interesting question: Can Satan read our thoughts? I grew up hearing from Sunday School and seminary teachers that he cannot. But I'm not so sure that this is correct. Let's consider the arguments on both sides of this question.

Arguments for Believing Satan Cannot Read Our Thoughts

To the best of my knowledge, the belief that many members have that Satan cannot read our thoughts comes from two sources:

1. Doctrine and Covenants 6:16: "Yea, I tell thee, that thou mayest know that there is none else save God that knowest thy thoughts and the intents of thy heart." This would seem to clearly tell us that *only God* can know the thoughts and intents of our hearts.
2. In 1987, Elder James E. Faust said that Satan "***cannot know our thoughts unless we speak them***."[11]

Many members point to the scripture above, as well as this quote from President Faust to say that we are safe—that Satan does not know our thoughts. However, before we sign off on that belief, let's consider the arguments for the other side.

Arguments for Believing Satan Can Read Our Thoughts

If we look up the above scripture (Doctrine and Covenants 6:16) in the *History of the Church*, we find that Joseph and Oliver apparently interpreted this passage very differently than most members of the Church. They understood it to mean that other human beings cannot know our thoughts. After quoting the entire revelation in full, the Prophet Joseph Smith, speaking of Oliver, says, "He knew that the

11. Faust, "Great Imitator," 35; emphasis added.

work was true, because **no being LIVING** knew of the thing alluded to in the revelation, but God and himself."[12]

From what Joseph himself said about this, it would appear that he and Oliver did not necessarily interpret that scripture to be speaking of the adversary but regarding people here in mortality. In addition, in *Teachings of the Prophet Joseph Smith*, Joseph says, "The spirits of the just are exalted to a greater and more glorious work; hence they are blessed in their departure to the world of spirits. Enveloped in flaming fire, they are not far from us, and **know and understand our thoughts, feelings, and motions** and are often pained therewith."[13]

This quote makes it even more clear that Joseph Smith did not interpret the passage in Doctrine and Covenants 6:16 the same way that many of us have. He seemed to recognize that spirits on the other side of the veil do indeed know our thoughts, feelings, and motions (although I wonder if the word "motions" was actually meant to be "emotions"). So, when the scripture said that "none else save God that knowest thy thoughts," why would Joseph say that the spirits of the just "know and understand our thoughts"? It is because he believed the scripture was only to be interpreted that no living person on earth knows our thoughts. And, since spirits are all governed by the same rules, if the spirits of the just know and understand our thoughts, it would seem very possible—if not probable—to expect that the spirits of the unjust can, as well.

Speaking further to this point, in the *Journal of Discourses*, Elder Orson Pratt says, "For instance; how do you suppose that spirits after they leave these bodies, communicate one with another? Do they communicate their ideas by the actual vibrations of the atmosphere the same as we do? I think not."[14]

Elder Pratt raises a very interesting question: How do spirits in the spirit world communicate? It seems that vocal cords made of spirit matter would have very little effect on physical molecules of air and that physical molecules of air would have very little impact upon tympanic membranes made of spirit matter.

---

12. Smith, Joseph, *History of the Church*, 1:35; emphasis added.
13. Smith, Joseph, *Teachings of the Prophet*, 337; emphasis added.
14. Young, *Journal of Discourses*, 3:100.

So how do spirits in the spirit world communicate? We know that a great many people who have had near-death experiences—who feel that they actually visited the spirit world—report that they communicated by thought while they were in the spirit world. This makes sense to me. We know that we can communicate with our Heavenly Father this way. We also know that this is how the Holy Ghost communicates with us. As we have already addressed, when we receive personal revelation, it most often comes to us in the form of thoughts that come to our mind and heart—*Bings!* And, similarly, Satan tempts us by putting thoughts into our mind and heart.

Note the following passage from the Doctrine and Covenants: "And, on this wise, the devil has sought to lay a cunning plan, that he may destroy this work; ***for he hath put it into their hearts to do this***, that by lying they may say they have caught you in the words which you have pretended to translate" (Doctrine and Covenants 10:12–13; emphasis added). Additionally, Elder Joseph Fielding Smith taught, "We should be on guard always to resist Satan's advances. . . . ***He has power to place thoughts in our minds*** *and to whisper to us in unspoken impressions to entice us to satisfy our appetites or desires* and in various other ways he plays upon our weaknesses and desires."[15] And, as we read earlier from 2 Nephi 28:22, "And thus he **whispereth in their ears**, until he grasps them with his awful chains, from whence there is no deliverance" (emphasis added).

So we know that Satan can put thoughts into our hearts. And if he *talks* to us in the same way that the Holy Ghost does—*by putting thoughts into our mind and heart*—does it not make sense that he would *listen* to us in the same way—that our thoughts would be heard by him?

If Satan ***can*** read our thoughts, he would certainly like nothing better than for us to think that he ***cannot*** read them. If he could, and we believed that he couldn't, wouldn't it give him a great advantage over us? If we thought that he can't read our thoughts, we would logically conclude that any answer that we receive to a prayer that was prayed in silence must necessarily be from the Lord because, after all, Satan cannot read our thoughts. Yet, I'm sure that many

---

15. Smith, Joseph Fielding, *Answers to Gospel Questions*, 3:81; emphasis added.

will recognize times when they were praying in silence and wrong or bad thoughts came to them. Why do you think that was? It was not a coincidence, nor, typically, was it their own thoughts. They were thoughts that were placed there by Satan. It would seem that the safest course of action is to assume that Satan is somehow discovering what your thoughts are and to be very careful.

Elder ElRay L. Christiansen wrote, "Satan knows all the tricks. He knows where we are susceptible to temptations and how to entice us to do evil. He and his messengers suggest evil, minimize the seriousness of sin, and make evil inviting. . . . **Surely then Satan and his followers have some knowledge of our thoughts and tendencies.** . . . Satan and his aides no doubt may know our inclinations, our carnal tastes and desires."[16]

Don't Underestimate Satan

I didn't want to show only one side of the argument, so I pointed out the arguments on both sides. Through my studying, I believe it is safer to work under the assumption that somehow Satan can perceive what we are thinking. By so doing, we will be better prepared to combat the adversary. But what about President Faust's quote that Satan can't read our thoughts? As an Apostle, he was a prophet, seer, and revelator. Like you, I like to accept the words of the prophets as truths. However, even accepting that quote as truth, we need to remember that when Satan is giving us a prompting immediately after a prompting from the Holy Ghost, it is not necessarily our thought he is reading. Rather, he is acting on what he just heard the Holy Ghost prompt us to do. So, even if he can't know our thoughts, since he is a spirit and can communicate as spirits do, just by being around us, he can hear what the Holy Ghost tells us and quickly work to tell us why that prompting doesn't make sense.

Even if Satan can't know our thoughts directly, he has enough knowledge of them to accomplish his purposes. And, because of this, we need to always be on guard. We should work under the assumption that Satan has more than just a *pretty good idea* of what we are thinking.

---

16. Christiansen, "Read Our Thoughts," 49; emphasis added.

In the July 1984 *Ensign*, we read, "**It is possible that Satan can at least determine our susceptibility to a particular temptation from our words and actions, which reveal our thoughts**. . . . Satan can see our fruits as well as any person—and we can be certain that he'll be quick to take advantage of the weaknesses we exhibit."[17]

Understanding 1 Corinthians 10:13 Better

Although 1 Corinthians 10:13 tells us that we won't be tempted above what we are able, I worry that too many members may "relax" when they read that scripture and feel that they are safe. Please note that the way it tells us that God will keep us from being tempted above what we are able is that He will "make a way to escape." Could it be that, if we are not in tune with the Spirit, we may not know about the way to escape, and the temptation may indeed become too much for us? With this in mind, let's review what Alma taught: "But that ye would ***humble yourselves before the Lord, and call on his holy name, and watch and pray continually, that ye may not be tempted above that which ye can bear, and thus be led by the Holy Spirit***, becoming humble, meek, submissive, patient, full of love and all long-suffering" (Alma 13:28; emphasis added). It seems evident that Alma is warning us that it isn't as simple as assuming that we will not be tempted above what we can bear. We have a responsibility to fulfill in order to keep it that way.

Let's consider an example from our own lives that can help us see how, no matter what, Satan probably knows our thoughts a lot more than we may think. Let's assume you are a parent and you tell your teenage daughter to do something that you know she disagrees with. When you do, she makes a face. She doesn't say anything, but because of what you previously already know about her feelings on the subject, as well as by the face she is making, you have a very good idea about what she is thinking. If we, with the limited experience we have had on earth, can ascertain thoughts fairly easily from what we know and what we observe, how well do you think the adversary can ascertain our thoughts? Remember, he never had to pass through

17. Peterson, "Perceive Our Thoughts?" 31; emphasis added.

the veil of forgetfulness, so he has known each of us very well for millennia—and he has had thousands of years to practice his craft, becoming better all the time at figuring out what we are thinking. In fact, Elder James E. Faust said that he once heard the following quote from Ernest LeRoy Hatch, who had been serving as the president of the Guatemala City Temple: "The devil is not smart because he is the devil; he is smart because he is old."[18] This should help us understand that, knowing us as he does (one could argue that he may even know us better than we know ourselves)—and with countless years of practice—he has gotten pretty good at knowing what we are thinking.

If it is true that all spirits communicate in the same way, it would make sense that, even if Satan can't read our thoughts, when the Holy Ghost is communicating to us, Satan—or one of his followers—can hear what the Holy Ghost is telling us. That is why (and how) he can jump in immediately afterward and try to convince us not to do what the Holy Ghost just told us to do (the next chapter is on this very subject). As a result, we should still be careful about thinking that if we pray in silence, we are "safe." After all, since he can hear the response from the Holy Ghost to our prayer—and we know that he can put his thoughts into our minds—it only makes sense that we should expect him to try to confuse us with doubts to the answers we get from the Holy Ghost.

It is *quite clear* that the adversary *can* and *does* put thoughts into our minds. He is constantly trying to "prompt" us with *Bings!* of his own—and hoping we will not realize that those promptings are from him. He knows that, once we realize that his promptings are from him, we will not follow those promptings.

Do Not Give Up Hope

It is important to remember what Joseph Smith taught: "**All beings who have bodies have power over those who have not**."[19] We are in a much stronger position than Satan and his followers. Do not ever lose hope. And remain close to the Spirit to help protect you

18. Faust, "Great Imitator," 35.
19. Smith, Joseph, *Teachings of the Prophet*, 185; emphasis added.

from the adversary and all of his tricks. In fact, in 1 Nephi 22:26, we read, "And because of the righteousness of his people, Satan has no power. . . . for **he hath no power over the hearts of the people, for they dwell in righteousness**" (emphasis added). The secret of our success, then, is to live righteously and have the Spirit with us.

You Aren't Bad If You're Getting Promptings from the Adversary

One of the first times that I taught a group of youth about getting promptings (from the Holy Ghost and from the adversary), one of the youth asked, "What can I do to live a better life so that I won't get his promptings?" I explained that this wasn't how it worked. But, ever since then, I have noticed that there are always people who hear this message and worry that they must be doing something wrong in their lives that is allowing the adversary in. My answer to that is *absolutely not*! Let's prove it with a quote and a couple of examples that should dismiss any doubt on the matter.

Elder Jeffrey R. Holland, in a BYU devotional address on March 2, 1999, said the following: "There is a lesson in the Prophet Joseph Smith's account of the First Vision that virtually everyone in this audience has had occasion to experience, or one day soon will. It is **the plain and very sobering truth that before great moments, certainly before great spiritual moments, there can come adversity, opposition, and darkness. Life has some of those moments for us, and occasionally they come just as we are approaching an important decision or a significant step in our life**."[20]

What are the details of what happened to Joseph? As a fourteen-year-old boy, he went to a grove of trees near his home—that we now refer to as the Sacred Grove—in order to offer up a prayer to his Heavenly Father, with a desire to know which church he should join. We remember that this was when he had what we call the First Vision—as he was visited by Heavenly Father and Jesus Christ. It was this vision that changed the world forever. But what we don't hear

20. Holland, "Confidence"; emphasis added.

about nearly as much is what happened right before they appeared. In Joseph Smith—History 1:15–17, we read as follows:

> I kneeled down and began to offer up the desires of my heart to God. I had scarcely done so, when immediately I was seized upon by some power which entirely overcame me, and had such an astonishing influence over me as to bind my tongue so that I could not speak. Thick darkness gathered around me, and it seemed to me for a time as if I were doomed to sudden destruction. But, exerting all my powers to call upon God to deliver me out of the power of this enemy which had seized upon me, and *at the very moment when I was ready to sink into despair and abandon myself to destruction—not to an imaginary ruin, but to the power of some actual being from the unseen world, who had such marvelous power as I had never before felt in any being—just at this moment of great alarm,* I saw a pillar of light exactly over my head, above the brightness of the sun, which descended gradually until it fell upon me. It no sooner appeared than I found myself delivered from the enemy which held me bound (emphasis added).

I know this is a rhetorical question, but was Joseph a bad person? Was that the reason that the adversary "got to him"? We all know that this was not the case. He was as good a fourteen-year-old boy as there ever was on the earth. The adversary didn't do what he did to him because he was bad. It was just the opposite. Satan wanted to destroy him—or, at the very least, get him to give up his attempt to ask God for help. From this story, we learn that we don't get a "free pass" to avoid Satan just because we are living good lives and trying to do the right thing.

An even better example is taken from the life of the only perfect man to ever walk the earth. In Matthew 4:2–3, we read, regarding our Savior, Jesus Christ, "And when he had fasted forty days and forty nights, he was afterward an hungered. And when the tempter came to him, he said, If thou be the Son of God, command that these stones be made bread." The scripture continues, showing how Satan continued to tempt Jesus. Was there something wrong with our Savior to have this happen to Him? Of course not. He was just about to begin

His ministry, and Satan was doing whatever he could to try to keep that from happening.

We need to remember that it is not only right *before* great things happen that the adversary will come to us. He also will attack us immediately *after* great events. In the example of Jesus above, it was right *after* a forty-day fast—and right *before* his mortal ministry was to begin.

We can read in Moses 1 of the great vision that God gave Moses. But that vision was immediately followed by the adversary appearing unto him and telling him to worship him. As you read of this experience, you will see that it was indeed a scary experience for Moses. This is how the adversary often works. And it's why so many new members of the Church fall away soon after baptism. They have a wonderful spiritual experience, but then Satan does all he can to get them to feel that it was a mistake. He will do the same to each of us after many spiritual experiences or answers to prayers that we will get. We need to refuse to listen to him and carry forward in what we know to be true.

From these examples, it is evident that no one should interpret being prompted by the adversary to mean you are a "bad person." In fact, it is much more likely—based on the examples above—that you are a good person, and Satan is trying to keep something really good from happening. He knows that you are about to change somebody's life—yours or the life of someone else—and he is simply trying to knock you off course. You should take it as a compliment that he is trying to stop you. Ignore him and keep following the Holy Ghost.

Both Elder Boyd K. Packer and his brother Leon served in the war. Elder Packer said his brother taught him that "the flak is always the heaviest closer to the target."[21] What Leon Packer said to his brother makes a lot of sense. And it is also very much in line with what the above examples show us. The adversary will try to attack us just prior to some significant spiritual event (to keep us from allowing it to happen) and just after one happens (to prevent it from having the impact that it would otherwise have on us). Either way, it is when we are "closer to the target."

---

21. Packer, "Spirit of Revelation," 24.

This idea also helps us understand an important part of Lehi's dream from 1 Nephi 8. As you will recall, the adversary attacked people in two different situations: First, as soon as they started on their path toward the tree, the mist of darkness arose to keep them from reaching the tree. Then, for those who reached the tree and ate of the fruit, he worked on them to be ashamed and embarrassed and get them to wander off. So it is with us. When the adversary is attacking us, it is oftentimes because we are just about to have some significant spiritual event in our lives—or we've just had one and he wants us to quickly lose the impact of it. *Always* be on guard.

The clearest explanation of how this principle works was taught to us by the Prophet Joseph Smith: "**The nearer a person approaches the Lord, a greater power will be manifested by the adversary to prevent the accomplishment of His purposes**."[22] Who would know this better than the Prophet Joseph? Doesn't that ring true to you? Those who are getting the closest to the Savior will have the strongest challenges from the adversary as he attempts to knock them off course. Because of his key role in the restoration of the gospel on the earth, we know that Joseph had a lot of experience with the adversary.

The author C. S. Lewis felt similarly. He wrote: "A silly idea is current that good people do not know what temptation means. This is an obvious lie. Only those who try to resist temptation know how strong it is. . . . You find out the strength of a wind by trying to walk against it, not by lying down."[23] I love this profound thought.

Finally, we need to remember that the prompting of the adversary is not going to have any effect on us unless we allow it to. For, just like the Holy Ghost's promptings, the adversary can only bring his promptings *unto* us. It is *up to us* to decide if we allow his promptings to come *into* our hearts. That is why this chapter, as well as this entire section, have been prepared—to help us recognize Satan's promptings much more easily and reject them. This reminds me of a great poem from an unknown author, titled "All the Water in the World." It goes like this:

---

22. Whitney, *Heber C. Kimball*, 146; emphasis added.
23. Lewis, *Mere Christianity*, 142.

All the water in the world,
However hard it tried,
Could never sink the smallest ship
Unless it gets inside.
And all the evil in the world,
The blackest kind of sin,
Can never hurt you the least bit
Unless you let it in.[24]

Never let the adversary into your life. Too often, one can make the mistake of thinking, "Just this one little thing won't matter." The adversary is happy to take that one small step in the wrong direction with you for now. He is very patient, especially because experience has told him that those very small steps will lead to more—and bigger—steps to come. We need to *keep him out*. His promptings will always come. This is why our prophets have told us that we must endure to the end. Even they—the Lord's Apostles—work on this for themselves. They know that the adversary never rests in his efforts against any of us.

Five Facts to Remember about Satan's Promptings

Now that we know that the adversary talks to us in the same way as the Holy Ghost—by prompting us with thoughts that pop into our head (*Bings!*)—it's important to learn how to avoid listening to his promptings. The following are five ways to quickly determine if promptings are from Satan. I'll first list these five facts, and then we will go into a little more detail about each one of them:

1. Satan won't prompt you to do good.
2. Satan is usually the second voice (or second prompting).
3. Satan uses great logic with his promptings.
4. Satan wants you to believe that his promptings are your own thoughts.
5. Satan oftentimes will speak to you in the first person.

---

24. Lyon, *Best-Loved Poems*, 302.

Fact 1: Satan Won't Prompt You to Do Good

Earlier in this book, we looked at Doctrine and Covenants 11:12, where the Lord tells us, "And now, verily, verily, I say unto thee, put your trust in that Spirit which leadeth to do good—yea, to do justly, to walk humbly, to judge righteously; and this is my Spirit." Just as we learned that this is a good way to identify that the *Bing!* we got was really from God, we can use that same test to see if a prompting is from the adversary. If we are prompted to do evil, we can know *immediately* that the prompting is from the adversary and *not* from God.

Mormon makes this even clearer for us. In Moroni 7:17, he says, "But whatsoever thing persuadeth men to do evil, and believe not in Christ, and deny him, and serve not God, then ye may know with a perfect knowledge it is of the devil; for after this manner doth the devil work, for he persuadeth no man to do good, no, not one; neither do his angels; neither do they who subject themselves unto him."

With help from these two verses, we should easily be able to distinguish between the two different types of *Bings!* (or promptings)—the ones that come from the Holy Ghost and those that come from the adversary. Satan will either prompt us to do wrong or, at the very least, he will prompt us to *not* do the good that we were just prompted by the Holy Ghost to do. And that leads us to the next point.

Fact 2: Satan Is Usually the Second Voice (or Second Prompting)

Earlier, we quoted Joseph Smith as having said, "If you will listen to the first promptings, you will get it right nine times out of ten." In addition, Elder Ronald A. Rasband said, "We must act on the *first* prompting. . . . We must be confident in our first promptings. . . . First promptings are pure inspiration from heaven."[25] Neither Joseph nor Elder Rasband—nor any other Church leader over the years—would have spoken about the first prompting if there was no second prompting. If there was not a second prompting, they would have only said to "follow the promptings" instead of referring to the first prompting. Therefore, it only makes sense that we should expect another

25. Rasband, "Holy Spirit Guide," 95–96.

prompting that will often come *after* that first prompting. I often refer to it as the second voice.

Since we know that the Holy Ghost is the first prompting, the question is, who is the second prompting? It is the person who wants us to ignore—or not act on—the first prompting. It is indeed the adversary. It can only be him. While it is true that Satan can also be a first prompting, he is not nearly as dangerous when he is acting in that role because when he is a first prompting, he is *always* prompting us to do evil. In those cases, it is extremely easy to recognize him and his promptings for what they are as soon as they come to us. Typically, in those cases, he will tempt us to do or say things that we know to be wrong, such as to be mean to someone, partake of something we shouldn't, or participate in something we should avoid. In those cases, as long as we are living as we should and have the Holy Ghost with us, his promptings should be much easier to recognize and avoid. Elder Packer put it very plainly for us when he said, "If ever you receive a prompting to do something that makes you *feel* uneasy, something you know in your *mind* to be wrong and contrary to the principles of righteousness, do not respond to it!"[26] That is very simple counsel to follow that will keep us safe when bad first promptings come to us.

However, when the adversary is acting as the second voice—or second prompting—as he is so often in our lives, he is *far* more dangerous. He is also much more difficult to recognize. You see, when he is the second prompting, his message will usually come *immediately on the heels* of that first prompting from the Holy Ghost, and he will try to convince us to *not* do what the Holy Ghost just got through prompting us to do. He does not want us to act on those promptings from the Holy Ghost, so he—or one of his followers—will be there to jump right in after we get a prompting from the Holy Ghost and give us a very good reason to *not* act on the prompting we just got. He is especially good at this because of the next technique of his.

Fact 3: Satan Uses Great Logic with His Promptings

This topic is so important that I have dedicated the entire next chapter to it. As a result, we won't spend time talking about it at this

26. Packer, "Personal Revelation," 61.

point other than to point out that it is one of the most successful strategies that he uses. Stay tuned for more on this important fact in our next chapter!

Fact 4: Satan Wants You to Believe That His Promptings Are Your Own Thoughts

The adversary wants us to believe that the promptings we get from the Holy Ghost are our own thoughts so that we won't think they are as important as we would if we knew that they were truly coming from a member of the Godhead. He knows that if we think they are our own thoughts, we won't give them the same level of importance. It will be much more likely that we will procrastinate acting on the thought—even if we think those thoughts were good ideas. And, by putting them off, there is a good chance we will not remember to act on them later. The Holy Ghost, however, wants us to know that the promptings are from him.

Interestingly, not only does the adversary want us to think that the promptings we receive from the Holy Ghost are our own thoughts, he *also* wants us to believe that the promptings from *him* are our own thoughts. Unlike how we will act if we know a prompting is from the Holy Ghost, Satan knows that if we recognize a prompting as being from him, we will not even consider acting on it. Therefore, Satan wants us to think that promptings from him are our own thoughts. And, with the logic that he uses—which we will discuss in the next chapter—many people are fooled into thinking that it is just their own thought. We need to make every effort to recognize the *Bings!*—or promptings—from the adversary as being from him.

With that said, let's remember what Joseph Smith said in the quote that we used to open this chapter: "Nothing is a greater injury to the children of men than to be under the influence of a false spirit **when they think they have the Spirit of God**."[27] So, while Satan will almost always work to get us to believe that his promptings are actually our own thoughts, it is important to note that he can also work to have us believe that his prompting is really a prompting from the Holy Ghost. And, as Joseph said,

---

27. Smith, Joseph, *Teachings of the Prophet*, 211; emphasis added.

that is when he is the absolute most dangerous. Joseph was acutely familiar with many such situations. We can point to many, but we will use just one as an example—the events that led up to Doctrine and Covenants 28.

Hiram Page, one of the eight witnesses to the gold plates, obtained a seer stone and began receiving what he honestly believed were revelations concerning such things as the establishment of Zion and Church hierarchy. There were many people who began to believe the "revelations" that he was getting. Joseph was alarmed at what was happening. He prayed to know what to do. In verse 11 of section 28, the Lord revealed to Joseph "that those things which [Hiram Page] hath written from that stone are not of me and that Satan deceiveth him." After Joseph received and shared this revelation, it required the humility of many people to see the error of their ways and repent. To Hiram's credit, he even had his seer stone destroyed. But this serves as a great example of how, if we are not careful, we can even be deceived by the adversary into believing that his promptings are from the Lord.

Fact 5: Satan Often Speaks to Us in the First Person

This is possibly one of the most dangerous tactics that the adversary uses. He has been successful to some degree with almost everyone in doing this. He has, in fact, destroyed many lives by talking to them in the first person—in his efforts to get them to believe it really was their own thought so that they would take ownership of it. Because this is such an important topic, we will go into more detail about it in an upcoming chapter.

Do We Ever Have Our Own Thoughts?

After I taught these principles to a group of people, a man said to me, "Wait a minute. If God can talk to us through the Holy Ghost, and those communications will seem like my own thoughts—and Satan can also talk to us, and his promptings will also seem like my own thoughts—is there even room for me to ever have my own thoughts? It almost seems like you are saying that every thought in my head is either from God or from Satan. You make it sound like I never do any of my own thinking."

My response to him was along these lines: Of course, we all do our own thinking as well. Every one of us will have our own thoughts. But, since our thoughts are shaped by our experiences and beliefs, it is important to note which promptings we have been following. Those promptings will help shape the direction of our own thoughts. For example, after someone has continued to make bad choices time after time, Satan no longer needs to invest as much time or effort on that person because of the confidence he has that this person will continue to make bad choices on his or her own. On the other hand, someone who continually follows the promptings of the Holy Ghost will begin to create habits of making right choices. His or her thoughts will naturally be in line with what the Holy Ghost would prompt that person to do. In this case, as promptings continue to get easier to recognize, the person's own thoughts will automatically move toward right courses of action. So the question really is, "Are your own thoughts leading you to do good?" If not, it is either because (1) your thoughts are really promptings from the adversary, or (2) you are doing the adversary's bidding for him and making his job a whole lot easier because you are thinking of bad things all on your own.

We need to strive to always have our thoughts aligned with what God would want and what the Holy Ghost would inspire us to do. Isn't that part of what Christ meant when He taught us that He and the Father are "one"? We should work hard to align our will and our thoughts with God's. I've always found it simpler to just assume that any good or positive thought is from God. I feel it is safer to give Him the credit. On the other hand, by assuming that all negative thoughts come from the adversary, I am less likely to listen to or act on them.

Now that we have briefly explained each of the five important facts that we should always remember about the adversary and his promptings, the next few chapters will go into more detail about some of these facts.

CHAPTER 4

Beware of the Logic of the Second Voice

"When we receive an impression in our heart, we can use our mind either to rationalize it away or to accomplish it. Be careful what you do with an impression from the Lord."

—Richard G. Scott[1]

As stated earlier, the adversary is the most dangerous when he is the second voice—the second prompting that we receive. In those instances, we can easily be fooled into not recognizing that the prompting is actually from him. Sometimes, we may believe that it is our own thought. Worse still, we may even think that it is the Holy Ghost giving us some advice or a warning. Because this works so well for him, it is the strategy that Satan will most often use with people who are honestly trying to live their lives the right way.

It may be hard to believe that the adversary could actually give us a prompting that we would ever confuse with having been from the Holy Ghost, but our own Church leaders have tried to warn us that this is possible. Besides the quote from Joseph Smith and the example from Hiram Page's life that we shared earlier, Elder Robert D. Hales, not long before he passed away, told us in his April 2016 general conference address that "sometimes the adversary tempts us with false

1. Scott, "Learning to Recognize Answers," 31.

ideas that we may confuse with the Holy Ghost."[2] It is *critical* that we consider how he does this so that we can better avoid being fooled by him and his promptings. It is for this very reason that the prophet Mormon admonishes us in Moroni 7:14: "Wherefore, take heed, my beloved brethren, that ye do not judge that which is evil to be of God, or that which is good and of God to be of the devil."

The first voice (when it is prompting you to do or say something good) is always from the Holy Ghost. This voice will encourage us to do or say something that will bless the life of someone—at times, even ourselves. However, many times, right after that first voice—or first prompting—comes to us, that dangerous second voice will pop into our heads. And it will come, most often, *immediately* following that first prompting from the Holy Ghost, trying to quickly persuade us *not* to do what the first voice just told us we should do. Satan wants us to "shoot down" the prompting from the Holy Ghost before we even consider acting on it.

When the adversary is acting as that second voice, not only will he come in right on the heels of that first prompting, but he will also use another tactic that is extremely effective for him. He will use *logic* in his prompting in order to convince us *not* to say or do that good thing that the Holy Ghost just prompted us to do or say. And let me warn you, *his logic is extremely good*! Honestly, I don't think there is anyone that can come close to the adversary when it comes to his successful use of great logic. Because of his logical reasoning, you will almost always feel like it makes sense *not* to act on what the Holy Ghost just prompted you to do. Many times, just as Elder Scott mentioned in the quote at the beginning of this chapter, it's common to "rationalize away" that first prompting. But I love how Elder Scott ended that quote: "Be careful what you do with an impression from the Lord." We must be stronger in our commitment to follow those first promptings when they come—and to avoid the logic of the second voice that comes to us.

Elder Marion G. Romney explained *why* we need to be so careful about what we do with impressions from God. He told us that "**Satan is irrevocably committed to countering and overcoming the influence of the Spirit of Christ upon men**. He is the representative,

2. Hales, "The Holy Ghost," 106.

promoter, and advocate of that 'opposition in all things' referred to by Lehi in his instructions to his son Jacob (See 2 Nephi 2:11, 14–18)."[3] That is his goal: "countering and overcoming" those first promptings that we get from the Holy Ghost. He simply doesn't want us to act on those promptings that come from God.

I could write an embarrassingly thick book about all of the times in my life that I fell for the logic of the second voice before I understood that Satan is indeed the second prompting and that he comes in *immediately* after the first prompting pops into our head, using his amazing logic to convince us *not to* do what the Holy Ghost just prompted us to do. Over and over again in my life, I have listened to that second voice instead of the first voice. *Why?* It wasn't because I was a bad person. I have always tried to be a good person. So why would a good person choose to follow a prompting from the adversary instead of a prompting from the Holy Ghost when they both came to that person at about the same time? It is because of the *amazing logic* that the adversary uses. It always makes *so much sense.* And, to make matters worse, it is usually an easier path to follow. As a result, we can easily fall into the trap of accepting his logic and using it to rationalize away that first prompting that we received.

The fact is, we have all fallen for his logic many times. As I point this out, please do not feel bad for having fallen for the logic of the adversary's promptings in the past. Rather, it is simply important to understand what he does—and how he does it—in order to recognize his promptings in the future and ignore them. As we begin to recognize his promptings, they will no longer keep us from acting on the promptings that we have been getting from the Holy Ghost.

Let's consider a few quick examples of the logic of the second (Satan's) voice:

Example 1: The "Warm Discussion" Between a Husband and Wife

This could happen with anyone—a husband and wife, a brother and sister, or even two friends. For the sake of this example, let's

3. Romney, "Great Deceiver," 36; emphasis added.

say it's a husband and wife. They're having a discussion that ends up getting rather heated. They're getting upset at each other and perhaps even exchange some unkind words. In this case, the wife decides to end the discussion and not allow the bad feelings that are growing between the two to get any worse. So she gets up and exits the room. As soon as she leaves the room, the husband has a thought that pops into his head (*Bing!*) that says, "I should apologize." However, immediately after having that thought pop into his head, he gets another thought that pops into his head (*Bing!*). This second *Bing!* says, "No. Why should I apologize for this argument? She started it!"

Which voice do you think most spouses would listen to in situations like this? That's right! Sadly, it's usually the second one. Now, where do you think those two thoughts came from? It's obvious, isn't it? That first thought—to go apologize and help bring peace and love back into their relationship—came from the Holy Ghost. The second prompting—to *not* do that—came from the adversary. He doesn't want the husband to make things better between himself and his wife; he wants to drive a bigger wedge between them.

Some readers will remember the example of a time when Joseph Smith was not able to translate the plates. When he went outside and prayed, it was made known to him that it was because of bad feelings he had with his wife, Emma. He went and asked her forgiveness and then was able to continue with the translation. Note that the story does not mention who "started it" or who was in the wrong. Simply the fact that there were bad feelings between the two kept him from having the Spirit with him to translate. Yes, in this example, it is very obvious who the first prompting was from.

This is a simple example, but little things like this *happen all the time in our lives*! And, just as God is in the very details of our lives, we need to recognize that—since the adversary wants to destroy our souls—he and his angels are also in those same details. That is why he will work against us even in seemingly small things. We need to be on the lookout for both the first *and the second* promptings and know to follow that first, positive prompting (and ignore the second one).

Example 2: The Missionaries and the Man on the Side of the Road

Let's consider a second example. Two hard-working missionaries from our church are walking down a street. They see a man standing on the sidewalk, talking on his cell phone and growing more and more agitated. One of the missionaries gets a *Bing!* from the Holy Ghost that pops into his head. He feels that he should stop and talk to the man. He even starts to walk toward the man, but as he does, he immediately gets another thought that pops into his head (*Bing!*). This thought says, "No. First of all, he is very busy on his cell phone. Second, he seems mad. If we stop and talk to him right now, he will just end up getting mad at us and not only won't talk to us, but he will also have worse feelings about our church and will probably never give any missionaries a chance in the future. This is bad timing. We just need to keep on walking."

In most situations, which voice will that good, well-intentioned missionary listen to and act on? Unfortunately, most often, in cases like this, he will listen to the second prompting. Why? Because *it makes so much sense.* It wasn't that the missionary wanted to do wrong. He wants to do the right thing. However, there was such *outstanding logic* in what that second *Bing!* told him. He didn't want to be the reason that this man would never talk to missionaries in the future—all because two overzealous missionaries interrupted him at a terrible time.

In this case, those two great missionaries kept on walking. What happened in reality? They missed a wonderful opportunity to talk to a man that the Holy Ghost *knew* they should talk to. God was trying to get the missionaries to stop and talk to him. The missionary should have ignored the second voice. He should have continued to act on that *first* prompting.

Example 3: The Member of the Church and the Nonmember Friend

Here is a third example. You have a non-member friend at your house, and you get a prompting (*Bing!*) that you should invite her to your ward activity this Friday night. But immediately after that prompting, you get another *Bing!* that says, "No. If I do, she'll think I have only been pretending to be her friend so I can convert her to our Church. I'd better not invite her. It could ruin our friendship!" And, just like almost every other member of the Church, you end up not inviting her to that activity. This is very sad because it was the Lord who was prompting you to invite your friend to this activity. But the adversary won out by using the "fear of losing a friendship" strategy. This is an extremely successful trick he uses to make sure we keep our mouths closed when it comes to sharing the gospel.

As we read earlier, Elder Robert D. Hales said, "Sometimes the adversary tempts us with false ideas that we may confuse with the Holy Ghost."[4] We could cite many examples in which this has happened, but the one above is a classic. We may think that it is the Holy Ghost who is "saving us" from destroying a friendship that the Lord doesn't want to see ruined because He wants you to eventually help this friend join the Church. However, it was *not* the Holy Ghost that was talking to you. The Holy Ghost was the *first* voice that prompted you to extend the invitation. Why would the Holy Ghost give you an impression to invite and then give you a reason not to do so?

On this note, at one time or another, I have lived in each of the following states in the United States: California, Wyoming, Nevada, Utah, Kansas, Ohio, and Massachusetts. In addition, I've spent a total of five years of my life in São Paulo, Brazil. You will note that, other than Utah, every place I have lived has been a place where members of the Church were definitely in the deep minority compared to the population at large. An interesting thing I've noticed as I have lived in those places is that members of every other church that I have come across are not afraid to invite people to their church meetings or activities. They simply invite their friends, and when a friend says "no," it doesn't bother them at all. Why are members of our Church the only ones who are afraid to invite people to church meetings or activities? Why do you think that is? The answer is easy. It is that second voice—that *Bing!*—from the adversary.

4. Hales, "The Holy Ghost," 106.

As a matter of fact, I have even talked to people who are converts to our Church who have shared with me that, prior to joining the Church—as members of their former church—they had no fear in inviting friends to attend their meetings or activities. Yet, after being baptized into our church, all of a sudden, they started being afraid to do the same thing that was so easy for them to do before. They have even asked me why I thought that was. I explained to them why. The adversary does not want us to help people become closer to making covenants with their Savior. We must always be observant and recognize the promptings of the adversary and the logic that he uses. He is very subtle, and he is an expert at using logic to convince us *not* to act on those first promptings from the Holy Ghost.

While we are on the subject of inviting our friends to church, I would like to share one more thing with you: You will *never* lose a friend over inviting them to church. That will virtually never happen. If anything, your friendship will usually grow from the invitation being extended—even if they say "no."

Think about it this way. Let's say you have a great friend of another religion who invites you to their services on an upcoming Sunday. Will you quit wanting to be their friend simply because they extended the invitation? Of course not. If anything, you may feel even better about your friendship that your friend would think so much about you that he or she would invite you to go to their church. Remember this the next time you have a second prompting that says, "Don't invite your friend to this church meeting/activity. It will hurt your friendship!"

His Logic Is Good and Can Even "Feel" Right

Elder Richard C. Edgley said, "So we ask ourselves, 'Who are we going to believe in our search for happiness and well-being?' Will it be Satan, the author of all lies and deceit, whose single objective is to destroy us? Or are we going to believe a loving Heavenly Father, who is the source of all truth and happiness, whose sole objective is rewarding us with His eternal love and joy?"[5]

---

5. Edgley, "Satan's Bag of Snipes," 43.

But he also warned in that same talk that, because the logic that the adversary uses makes so much sense, and for many other reasons, "Satan's lies can be very enticing."[6]

President Spencer W. Kimball wrote, "[Satan] will use his logic to confuse and his rationalizations to destroy."[7] Satan wouldn't use logic in his promptings to us if they didn't work. He has been *extremely successful with his logic for thousands of years.* We need to recognize this and *learn to ignore his promptings.*

Elder James E. Faust said, "Who has not heard and felt the enticings of the devil? **His voice often sounds so reasonable and his message so easy to justify**. It is an enticing, intriguing voice with dulcet tones. It is neither hard nor discordant. **No one would listen to Satan's voice if it sounded harsh or mean**. If the devil's voice were unpleasant, it would not entice people to listen to it."[8] Elder Gary E. Stevenson told us that "Satan, the father of lies and the great deceiver, would have us question things as they really are and either ignore eternal truths or replace them with something that appears more pleasing."[9]

You will note that, in each of the three examples above, the second prompting made a lot of sense and was, in fact, the "easier" path to follow. To follow the prompting from the Holy Ghost will almost always require us to be courageous and to step outside of our comfort zone. For that reason, when we get that second prompting that gives us a solid, logical reason to *not* act on what the Holy Ghost just told us to do, it seems to us to be just as Elder Stevenson says—"more pleasing" and thus, much easier to follow. The adversary will oftentimes give us *a logical reason to do nothing.* And, sadly, we have been buying into that for far too long.

God Does Not Need Logic

As we consider how the adversary will use great logic to convince us not to act on a prompting from the Holy Ghost, we need to

6. Edgley, 43.
7. Kimball, *Faith Precedes the Miracle*, 152.
8. Faust, "The Great Imitator," 34; emphasis added.
9. Stevenson, "Deceive Me Not," 94.

remember that *the Lord does not need logic.* He is a God of miracles. And, as such, He simply has no need for logic. When you know what the right answer is every time, who cares about logic? As a matter of fact, *oftentimes, the promptings from the Holy Ghost won't make logical sense.* When that happens, don't worry about it. Just act on them anyway. In fact, I have a testimony that God loves the crazies—those people who are not afraid to act on His promptings even when they don't make logical sense. We will get into this in more detail in an upcoming chapter. But for now, we should simply realize that as we begin to push ourselves to act on the promptings from the Holy Ghost no matter what, it will begin to be easier to act on them even when they don't seem to make sense.

Let's commit to follow every first prompting to do or say something positive. As we do, we will help the Lord bless our lives and the lives of many other people.

Do Not Act on Just Any Crazy Thought!

Before we go any further, let's be clear about what we are saying. We are *not* saying that you should act on any crazy thought that comes into your head. We are not condoning "craziness for the sake of craziness." Many people will have crazy thoughts of their own—or get crazy ideas from the adversary. We are *not saying* that we should just do any illogical thing. Rather, we are saying that we should not be afraid to act on promptings from the Holy Ghost—which will always be to do something positive or say something positive—just because it doesn't make logical sense to do so.

For example, I remember an interview I had with a missionary who shared with me the following experience. He and his companion were following up on a name in their area book. When they arrived at the house, the man saw them coming. He came out of his house smoking a cigarette and began to call them foul names. He was swearing and saying all kinds of bad things about the two missionaries and about the Church. These two great servants of God just wanted to leave and make a note in their area book about the man who lived at this address, warning any future missionaries that they should avoid this home at all costs. First, the missionaries apologized profusely that anyone from the Church had ever done anything to make him feel that way and apologized to him for any and all offenses that he had suffered from any member of the Church. Then, as they were leaving—and, as the man was feeling pretty proud of himself for what he had done to the missionaries—one of the missionaries felt prompted to tell the man that he was wrong to judge the whole Church by a few bad experiences. He also was prompted to bear a strong testimony of the Church. When the missionary was done, the man fell silent for the first time. He had a much different countenance. He said, "I'm not sure how you had the courage to say what you did. But I needed to hear that. I want you to come back and teach me whatever you have to teach me." *This* is the kind of "craziness" that God wants each of us to have—a commitment to boldly act on His promptings even when they don't make any sense at the time.

The Adversary Can Even Use Another Person to Act as His Voice

Many times, the second voice will come to us as a thought in our own mind. Sometimes, though, that prompting will be put into the mind of someone else—perhaps someone who is with us at the time or someone that we know and respect—and that person will end up innocently acting as the second voice by simply vocalizing the thoughts that will pop into his or her head. When this happens, don't feel negatively toward that person. They are merely voicing the prompting that came to them. Since we also get those thoughts many times, we shouldn't be upset at other people who get them as well. But we must recognize that this happens, and we must refuse to let anyone else keep us from acting on the promptings of the first voice.

President Joseph Fielding Smith said that the adversary **"will appear to us in the person of a friend or a relative in whom we have confidence.**"[10] Well-intentioned people—friends and family—can be used by the adversary to further his work against God's plan. It doesn't mean they are bad people. They are simply being fooled and vocalizing the *Bings!* that are coming to their minds. I have heard countless examples of our good missionaries and how one had a *Bing!*

10. Smith, Joseph Fielding, *Answers to Gospel Questions*, 3:81; emphasis added.

to do something or say something and their well-intentioned companion talked them out of it. Some have even said that the reason that they listened to their companion and did *not* act on that first prompting was that their companion voiced the same concern that had popped into their mind right before the companion said it. They considered that a second witness that they shouldn't act on that first prompting, when in reality, it is much more likely that it had been the adversary, acting as the second prompting and whispering to both missionaries right after that first prompting came.

"Never Suppress a Generous Thought"

In a BYU devotional on February 13, 2007, Sister Bonnie D. Parkin, former Relief Society General President, shared a wonderful story:

> Susan . . . was a wonderful seamstress. President [Spencer W.] Kimball lived in [her] ward. One Sunday, Susan noticed that he had a new suit. Her father had recently . . . brought her some exquisite silk fabric. Susan thought that fabric would make a handsome tie to go with President Kimball's new suit. So on Monday she made the tie. She wrapped it in tissue paper and walked up the block to President Kimball's home.
>
> On her way to the front door, she suddenly stopped and thought, 'Who am I to make a tie for the prophet? He probably has plenty of them.' Deciding she had made a mistake, she turned to leave.
>
> Just then Sister Kimball opened the front door and said, "Oh, Susan!"
>
> Stumbling all over herself, Susan said, "I saw President Kimball in his new suit on Sunday. Dad just brought me some silk from New York . . . and so I made him a tie."
>
> Before Susan could continue, Sister Kimball stopped her, took hold of her shoulders, and said: "Susan, never suppress a generous thought."[11]

---

11. Parkin, "Personal Ministry."

In a general conference talk where she reshared Bonnie Parkin's story, Sister Michelle D. Craig said,

> I love that! "Never suppress a generous thought." **Sometimes when I have an impression to do something for someone, I wonder if it was a prompting or just my own thoughts**. But I am reminded that "that which is of God inviteth and enticeth to do good continually; wherefore, every thing which inviteth and enticeth to do good, and to love God, and to serve him, is inspired of God." [Moroni 7:13] **Whether they are direct promptings or just impulses to help, a good deed is never wasted, for "charity never faileth"—and is never the wrong response**. Often the timing is inconvenient, and **we seldom know the impact of our small acts of service**. But every now and then, we will recognize that we have been instruments in the hands of God and we will be grateful to know that the Holy Ghost working through us is a manifestation of God's approval.[12]

We need to recognize that our "doubt"—when we wonder whether that first prompting was from the Holy Ghost or if it was our own thought—is not really a "doubt." Rather, it is that dangerous second prompting of the adversary that impresses us to doubt our promptings. Sister Craig's wonderful counsel on how to respond to those doubts was perfect. *Let's just act on our first promptings.*

The Woman Who Missed Church

Oftentimes, we will be fooled by the promptings of the adversary because, as he prompts us with that second voice (his *Bings!*), they will really feel like they are our own thoughts. Elder Robert D. Hales said, "All of us may be tempted to let our personal desires overcome the guidance of the Holy Ghost."[13] I wonder if one of the reasons he said that is he knew that, at times, we would be fooled into thinking that the adversary's promptings were our own thoughts. The following

12. Craig, "Divine Discontent," 54; emphasis added.
13. Hales, "The Holy Ghost," 106.

story is an example of how the adversary can get someone to believe that his prompting is their own desire or feeling and how it can bring sad results.

One of our very best missionaries from our mission, Sister Mariah Küster (now Dean), shared this story from her youth with me:

> When I was a teenager, I noticed that one of the new members in our ward was not there. We had met recently, and she was about 16 years older than me, but I thought she was such a nice person and we talked sometimes. **I had the distinct impression I should call her during the week and ask why she did not come.**
>
> I did not have her phone number and **I thought it would be really strange if I called her out of nowhere**, but the impression was so clear that I remember thinking about asking one of our friends in common for her phone number.
>
> I never did, and the following Sunday I saw her and thought about asking her why she was not there the past Sunday, **but again, I didn't, because I did not want to seem like I was gossiping**. She then turned to me and said: "Last Sunday, I did not come to church, because I wanted to know if anyone would notice, and nobody did."
>
> This broke my heart. I knew for sure it was not my own thought to reach out to her, but the Spirit guiding me. But I listened to the second voice and did not act on that first prompting and, as a result, it really hurt this wonderful new member.

It's easy to see in this story that the adversary uses great logic. He also gets us to think that his promptings are our own thoughts, which convinces us even further not to act on that first prompting. No wonder Elder Hales warned us not to let our "personal desires overcome the guidance of the Holy Ghost."

My Mom's Final Days and Her Funeral

I was blessed to be born into a wonderful family with great parents, Leonard and Davida Dalton. They were very special and did a great job raising their family. Our mom was especially amazing. Her father, Harry Lorenzo Payne, served as the temple president of the Mesa Arizona Temple when she was younger. Mom was always very close to the Spirit throughout her life. Our entire family, as well as many other people, learned a great deal from her. I will share some of those experiences later in this book. These next two stories are from the end of her life:

Story 1: The Spirit Told Her to Stay and Help Her Mom

The following story was shared by my youngest sister, Mindy Dalton Carter:

> My sisters and I were taking turns staying with our mom while she was in a rehab hospital after suffering a major stroke. One of the effects of the stroke was that she was unable to communicate. On one particular night, when both my sister and I were preparing to leave the hospital after staying with Mom for the day, I felt a distinct impression that I should stay the night with her. I knew that visiting hours were ending soon, and I was certain I would not be allowed to stay even if I asked for special permission, so I just ignored the feeling. But it came again, and this time it was stronger. I mentioned the feeling I had to my sister, and she too felt that there was no way I could stay the night with her after visiting hours had ended, so we both went back to our parents' house and went to bed.
>
> The next morning, when I arrived at the hospital to stay with Mom, my heart broke as I found her in bed crying and unable to tell me what had happened or why she was sobbing. The woman in the next bed informed me that Mom had gotten out of bed in the middle of the night and had taken a terrible fall. She said that the CNAs eventually came to turn off her alarm (meant to keep such incidents from happening),

and when they found her on the floor, they simply put her back in bed without checking to see if she had been injured. So she just lay in bed crying in pain the rest of the night with what we later discovered to be multiple broken bones.

I have never regretted so acutely not acting on a prompting as I did the moment I found my mom in tears. I wanted nothing more than to turn the clock back and do as I had been prompted to do. I learned a valuable and very difficult lesson that day.

Notice the following in her story:

1. The second prompting came *immediately* after the first prompting.
2. The second prompting made a lot of sense.
3. Her sister also innocently became the voice of that second prompting, voicing and "validating" the same thoughts that had already come to her from the second prompting.

Story 2: She Built Us a Rainbow

When our mom passed away shortly after Mindy's story above, it was hard for the whole family. She had been a spiritual anchor for all of us. She left behind her husband of fifty-six years, eleven children, and sixty-nine grandchildren. My twin brother, Len, was asked to speak at Mom's funeral. Although he had some prepared remarks, as he sat there, he felt impressed (*Bing!*) to add a bit to his talk about how much our mother loved rainbows. His thought was to tie into the story (and song) that had been popular years earlier called "I'll Build You a Rainbow," about a mom who was dying and her little boy. They were very close, and the little boy was scared and didn't want her to die. His mother told him that, on the other side, she would build him a rainbow, and every time he saw it, she wanted him to remember that his mother loved him. At her funeral, when his dad and this little boy were crying, the boy looked up and saw a big, beautiful rainbow. He got excited and told his dad that everything would be okay. Mom was still looking over them.

Immediately after getting that *Bing!* to share that story, Len had another thought pop into his head (*Bing!*) that told him the audience would find this story to be super corny. He remembers thinking that, although everyone knew Mom loved rainbows, they would probably think Len was making it about himself and that although the story had a tremendous impact on him, it wouldn't have any significance to the great majority of the funeral attendees. On top of that, it really didn't fit with the rest of his message. He ended up not including anything about rainbows in his talk.

Len's talk and the rest of the funeral went great. When it was over, we pall bearers started taking the coffin from the chapel to the hearse outside. As soon as we stepped outside, we saw a big, beautiful double rainbow that appeared to be ending right at our parents' house. All of us children knew that this was not a coincidence. We loved it and were blown away by the message Mom was sending us.

Len, on the other hand, was busy "beating himself up" that he didn't act on that first prompting. He told me that, during the following week, he saw rainbow after rainbow. To him, each one was just one more reminder to always act on the first prompting when it comes—and to ignore the second prompting.

Blessings That Come from Ignoring Satan's Promptings

Sister Ceci Lira, a wonderful sister missionary in our mission, shared the following story with me:

> It was late and it was hot. My companion (Sister Patricio) and I were walking to someone's house when a whisper of the Spirit reached our minds and hearts and made us pay attention to a man sitting on the street. This man was very dirty and extremely drunk. However, I could not deny that the prompting of the Spirit was very strong for us to invite this man to learn about the gospel. Yet, even with those strong promptings, the thoughts *immediately* came to me that, with him being so drunk, we would be "casting our pearls before swine." There was no way he would truly listen to our invitation. Even though that last thought was very strong, both

my companion and I remembered what our mission president said—that we needed to listen and act on the first prompting (the one that comes from the Spirit). With that teaching in mind, we had the courage to turn and talk to that man. To our great surprise, this drunk man listened to us and accepted our invitation to receive a gospel message in his home.

On the date we set, we went to his home. A tall boy, the man's nephew, opened the door. The boy was surprised that his uncle had invited us. He said that he didn't ever allow people to come to his home. And he wasn't even at home at that time. Even so, the nephew was very kind and introduced us to his mother, who invited us to enter. That day, we met six children and their mother. They heard our message, and that was the first of many times that we taught that family.

Soon, two of the girls and the boy who opened the door were baptized. Later, that same boy baptized two more of his brothers as well as a friend of his. After I came home from my mission, I found out that when that boy was old enough, he served a mission. And his family remains active to this day.

Sometimes I think about what would have happened if we had followed that second prompting and not spoken to that man. We probably would have felt sad only for a bit for not following the Spirit and then we would have forgotten that it had even happened. Or maybe not even have felt bad because he was so drunk that it wouldn't have been a good conversation. But, in reality, those children would not have ever known the gospel. And I would never have read that boy's words that he sent me, saying, "I wanted to thank you so much, Sister, for presenting the true gospel of Jesus Christ to me. Today, I really feel that the Savior is on my side. I love this gospel. Every moment in the church is incredible and I am very grateful."

Doubt the Doubts That Come after the First Prompting

During the October 2013 general conference, Elder Dieter F. Uchtdorf said something that has been quoted many times since:

"Doubt your doubts before you doubt your faith."[14] What a great message that is especially helpful when it comes to the many doubts that enter our minds after we get promptings from the Holy Ghost.

Elder William Mercês Silva served with so much faith in our mission! He shared the following wonderful experience with me:

> One day, my companion and I felt impressed to go to the home of the ward Relief Society president and offer to help her with anything she needed. She replied that she wanted me to bless her brother, who had been in a coma for three months and was being fed with a tube, living in a vegetative state. As soon as I laid my hands on that man, I felt that the Spirit commanded me to say the words that Christ used to the paralytic in the scriptures: "get up and walk." Immediately a second voice came to my mind, pointing out that the odds of this happening were not good, and the thought came strongly to me that "If it doesn't happen, this sister may lose her faith in the priesthood. I think it's better not to say those words."
>
> But then I felt that heavenly command once again, and I felt like God was telling me, "I am God. How can you say that you believe My words and then deny My power? If you are My representative, why don't you trust Me?"
>
> I was very nervous, but I said the Savior's famous words and ended the blessing. However, apparently nothing happened. The man did not get up. He stayed just as he had been for the previous three months. We said goodbye to the woman and left. I spent the whole week thinking about what happened. Was it just my desire to do some great miracle? Had it just been in my head? I probably was never supposed to even say those words. I felt terrible.
>
> When Sunday came, even though I was afraid to ask, I felt that I had to. So I went up to the Relief Society president to ask her how her brother was doing. She told me that it was a miracle. She said that, as soon as we left, her brother came out of the coma and got up and walked. I was very grateful

---

14. Uchtdorf, "Come, Join with Us," 23.

for this miracle. Then I began wondering why it happened the way that it did. Did the Lord need me to leave the home in order to perform the miracle because my lack of faith was restricting the Spirit? Or perhaps God wanted me to know that I can trust Him and follow the whisperings of the Spirit, even though I won't always know how it turns out, and I need to be okay with that—but that the important thing is that I do my part. Or maybe Heavenly Father just wanted to allow that family a more private moment for this wonderful miracle to occur. I am not sure. But what I do know is that I learned a very important lesson that day about trusting and acting on the promptings of the Holy Ghost and to not listen to the adversary in his role as the "second voice," trying to fill me with doubt.

Peter's Experience of Walking on Water

A story you will remember from your New Testament reading is a great way to summarize the message of this chapter. You will remember, in Matthew 14, the Apostles are in a boat when they see Jesus walking toward them on the sea. They think they are seeing a spirit and cry out in fear. In verse 27, Jesus replies, "Be of good cheer; *it is I;* ***be not afraid***" (Matthew 14:27; emphasis added). Peter then asks the Lord to bid him to come unto Him. Jesus does so with the simple invitation, "Come."

That single word gives Peter the confidence to jump out of the boat, and he begins walking toward the Savior on the sea. However, as he begins to see the winds and the waves, he starts to doubt, and we all remember what happens next. As he begins to sink, we read in verse 31: "And immediately Jesus stretched forth his hand, and caught him, and said unto him, *O thou of little faith,* ***wherefore didst thou doubt***?" (Matthew 14:31; emphasis added).

Peter's attempt at walking on water serves as a beautiful analogy of what the Lord is trying to teach us regarding our promptings from the Holy Ghost and how we should react to the doubts that the adversary will throw at us. Just as it was with Peter, if we want to have success, we need to ignore the adversary and "keep on walking."

When we first get the prompting from the Holy Ghost, we immediately want to respond in the same positive way that Peter did when the Savior said, "Come." That is when the adversary will throw everything he can at us—as he did with Peter—and, if we are not careful, our initial courage can be replaced with a mountain of doubts. In a figurative way, we will begin to sink.

As we read in Mormon 9:27, "***Doubt not, but be believing***" (emphasis added).

CHAPTER 5

Negative Self-Talk Is Not Self-Talk at All

"Because of Satan's deceit, we may at times feel unimportant, insignificant, or incapable."

—Elder Richard C. Edgley[1]

Previously, we addressed the fact that the adversary wants us to believe that the promptings we receive from the Holy Ghost as well as the promptings we get from him are our own thoughts. He knows that if we recognize that a prompting is really from the Holy Ghost, the likelihood that we will act on it is *much* higher than if we believe it is just our own thought. On the other hand, he also knows that if we recognize that his promptings are truly coming from him, we would never consider acting on them.

This is pretty interesting to think about. Because the Holy Ghost only speaks the truth, He has nothing to hide. However, the adversary is so full of deceit that not only does he not tell us the truth, but he doesn't even want us to know who is actually sending us the prompting!

Satan Has Had Years to Improve His Craft

Satan has been around for a very long time. Therefore, he has had years and years—*and years*—of experience, where he has learned which

1. Edgley, "Satan's Bag of Snipes," 43.

of his tricks work the best on us and which ones don't work quite as well. He also has a strong recollection of who we were before we came to earth, and knows our strengths and weaknesses from our pre-earth life. He uses all that he has learned over those many years against us. Elder Gary E. Stevenson emphasized this point when he said, "**[Satan] has spent millennia calculating and practicing the ability** to persuade God's children to believe that *good is evil* and *evil is good*."[2]

One of those methods that he has found to work *extremely* well is to talk to us in the *first person*—as if his prompting to us was really nothing more than us talking to ourselves ("self-talk," if you will). Instead of saying, "*You* shouldn't pray," for example, he will say, "*I* don't feel like praying tonight." He will repeat that same thought over and over, until we "take ownership of the thought." As he repeats that message over and over in our minds, we finally take ownership of it—meaning that we end up taking over for him and actually begin saying that same thought to ourselves because we believe that it was our thought in the first place.

Pride Versus Low Self-Esteem

Over the years, I have worked with a number of individuals who have fallen prey to Satan's methods. It has been my experience that two of Satan's greatest tools are at the complete opposite ends of the spectrum: On the one hand, he loves to get people to fall because of their *pride* or *ego*. And on the other hand, he attacks people's *self-esteem* and *self-worth*. It is interesting that these two methods which are at two opposite extremes have one very important thing in common: They both happen as a result of us ***comparing ourselves to others***. If Satan can get us to start comparing ourselves to others, he is well on his way to getting us to slip. And, once again, this is often aided by him talking to us in the first person as we do our comparing.

Rationalizing Sin Is Fake Self-Talk from the Adversary

The opening quote for this chapter was from a general conference address by Elder Richard C. Edgley. In that same talk, he shed light

2. Stevenson, "Deceive Me Not," 94; emphasis added.

on how the adversary puts thoughts into our minds to get us to justify wrong behavior or to rationalize the inaction of right behavior. Satan's goal is for us to think we are doing this rationalization ourselves in hopes that we will grab onto it as if it had been our idea all along. He wants us to think that these are *our* thoughts, that *we* are the ones thinking this way. Elder Edgley calls these promptings "clues" that will help us recognize when the adversary is talking to us. He shared some of them with us, specifically:

- "Everybody is doing it."
- "Nobody will know."
- "It is not really hurting anyone."
- "It won't hurt just this once."
- "So what?"

Elder Edgley also gave more examples, including the rationalization that you can later repent and still go on a mission or get married in the temple, or the rationalization that Christ paid the price for your sins and will still forgive you. Elder Edgley then said, "When such justifications are given either outright by others or subtly by the whisperings of the tempter, you are warned. Don't listen. Don't experiment. Just don't do it."[3]

Satan wants us to take ownership of his negative whispers and begin rationalizing further as to why it's okay to do those wrong things. And remember what President Spencer W. Kimball said about what Satan's rationalizations are targeted to do: "[Satan] will use his logic to confuse and his rationalizations to destroy."[4]

Some Fake Negative "Self-Talk" Whispers from the Adversary

Let's consider just a small sampling of the many other things Satan will say to us as he talks to us in the first person with his *Bings!* while he plays to our pride and ego or attacks our self-esteem:

---

3. Edgley, "Satan's Bag of Snipes," 43.
4. Kimball, *Faith Precedes the Miracle*, 152.

General Dangerous Promptings

- "That person brought those issues onto himself. If I help, I will just be enabling him."
- "I am not getting anything out of reading the scriptures."
- "I'm too tired to pray tonight."
- "I'm not sure if I believe this anymore."
- "I don't love my spouse. I don't want to be married anymore."

Pride/Ego Promptings

- "I am way smarter than him."
- "It will hurt my popularity if I continue to hang out with my old friends."
- "I would be embarrassed if I were dressed like her."

Low Self-Esteem/Poor Self-Worth Promptings

- "I'm fat."
- "I'm ugly."
- "Nobody likes me."
- "I am worthless."
- "Nobody cares about me."
- "I don't want to live anymore." (This is the most dangerous one of all.)

I can't say this strongly enough: We *must* finally start to recognize that negative self-talk is ***not "self-talk" at all***. At least, it never starts out that way. They are the whisperings of the adversary. Elder Edgley's quote at the beginning of this chapter said, "Because of Satan's deceit, we may at times feel unimportant, insignificant, or incapable." That is *exactly* what happens when we begin to take ownership of those thoughts. Unfortunately, it can quickly become real self-talk as we accept his "fake first-person" whispers to us and start to say the same thing to ourselves—taking over for him and his servants in doing his "dirty work" for him—of destroying our own self-esteem and self-worth and, eventually, our own lives. Satan has been far too successful with this strategy. We need to recognize these negative thoughts as being from him and cast them out as soon as they come to us.

The Most Dangerous Step

We do our best in defending ourselves against threats when we understand the goal of the enemy. We already know that the end goal of Satan is to destroy our souls. In that same talk by Elder Edgley, he warned, "Satan is the great deceiver, liar, and enemy to all that is good, including our happiness and our well-being. His great desire is to thwart our Heavenly Father's plan of happiness and make us 'miserable like unto himself' (2 Nephi 2:27)."[5]

When we think about this fake negative "self-talk" that the adversary engages in with us all the time, we should think about it with a full understanding of his end goal—he wants us to take ownership of these thoughts and begin thinking that way about ourselves. Why? Because he knows that as soon as we begin to think that way about ourselves, we accelerate the pace of decline in our morale and self-esteem. And, when our self-esteem declines, that is when we begin to make terrible decisions. ***Each step is carefully designed to simply lead us to the next step***. The enemy is very patient. He is okay if we just move one step closer to him—or one step farther away from God and the Holy Ghost—today.

Know that, with the adversary, **the most dangerous step is the first step!** Just by giving in and listening to *any* prompting of his at all, we are already on the wrong path. Our best defense is to *not listen to him at all!* Sister Michelle D. Craig said: "We can choose to walk the higher path that leads us to seek for God and His peace and grace, or we can listen to **Satan, who bombards us with messages that we will never be enough: rich enough, smart enough, beautiful enough, anything enough**. Our discontent can become divine—or destructive."[6] She makes it clear that there is only one choice that makes any sense.

---

5. Edgley, "Satan's Bag of Snipes," 43.
6. Craig, "Divine Discontent," 53; emphasis added.

I also love the counsel in James 4:7 in the New Testament: "Submit yourselves therefore to God. Resist the devil, and he will flee from you." The adversary can and will continue to try to attack us. We will need to be on the "lookout" for him until the end of our days. However, at the same time, if we continue to show him that we will not give him the smallest inch in his efforts with us—that we will block him out at the very start of every attempt—it only makes sense that he will choose to have his minions focus on someone else, where he can have more success.

Elder James E. Faust gave us the same message when he said, "However, we need not become paralyzed with fear of Satan's power. **He can have no power over us unless we permit it. He is really a coward, and if we stand firm, he will retreat**."[7] A great promise from an Apostle of God: "He is really a coward, and if we stand firm, he will retreat."

Whether the Message Is "You" or "I," It Is Still Coming from Him

Many people have shared with me that they have experienced all of these negative emotions that we have discussed, but some say that they don't ever remember it being a self-talk of "I" or "me." In their case, although the thoughts were just as terribly destructive, they came more as a "you" and "your" message. Looking back on it, they can now recognize that those promptings were still from the adversary. They felt at the time as though they were still having a conversation with themselves, telling themselves such things as "You don't deserve . . ." or "You're not worthy." Other people, however, told me that they actually thought it was the Holy Ghost or God telling them lies such as they weren't worthy to pray. It is extremely important that we recognize that it does not matter whether we get these negative messages in the first person or the second person; they all still come from the same destructive source. And in every case, he has the same goal in mind: the destruction of our self-esteem, which will take us farther down the path that leads to the destruction of our souls.

---

7. Faust, "Great Imitator," 35; emphasis added.

Speaking on this subject, Elder Boyd K. Packer said, "One of the adversary's sharpest tools is to convince us that we are no longer worthy to pray. **No matter who you are or what you may have done, you can always pray.**"[8] Elder Packer not only warned us that this kind of negative talk will come to us but that it is also one of the adversary's "sharpest tools." We need to remember that, as he promised, we can *always* pray!

Doubting the Words Given for a Priesthood Blessing

As an example of negative self-talk that can come to you as "you" and "your," I will share a story that happened to Elder Carson Burnside, another great, hard-working, humble missionary from our mission:

> One time, while serving in Riviera Paulista, I met with an active woman who was unable to walk more than a block before having to turn back to her house or simply fall down in the street. She said she wanted to come back to church but didn't think she could walk the seven or so very hilly blocks to the chapel. She asked us to give her a priesthood blessing so that she could have the strength to walk to and from church. As I prepared to give her the blessing, I felt very strongly that I should promise her that she would be able to walk every Sunday to church without fail. However, as soon as I put my hands on her head, I felt a very strong, cold and gloomy feeling and a voice that said, "You're not worthy enough to promise that. If you promise that and she still can't do it, then you're a fraud and your mission is worthless."
>
> Fortunately, just then, in my hour of doubt, I remembered a phrase from President Queiroz of the São Paulo Brazil Temple presidency. He said that we don't have to be perfect; we just need to be right in the eyes of the Lord. With a newfound confidence, I continued to promise her that she would have

8. Packer, "Prayer and Promptings," 45–46; emphasis added.

the ability to walk to church every Sunday. And, after that blessing, she never missed her Sunday meetings for the rest of the time that I served in that area.

Don't Get Down Because of Trials and Hardships

The adversary will also attack us and try to bring us down when we are faced with trials in our lives. We will all go through trials that we don't understand and, at times, may not even be sure that we have the strength to survive. Satan will jump at this opportunity and will try to capitalize on these tough times. He will try to convince you that this means that God does not really exist, or that, if He does exist, He sure doesn't love or care about you enough to protect you from these challenges. You will pray for relief, and, when it doesn't come immediately, Satan will attack again, trying to get you to stop believing in God. You may have thoughts like, "How could a God who really loves me allow something like this to happen?"

We must recognize that thoughts such as this are, once again, *Bings!* from the adversary. He will use every chance he can to get us to "give up on God." We must always remember that we were sent to earth to experience trials. It is our chance to show God that our faith is strong enough to get us through. We must live by faith. The reward that awaits us will outweigh our trials by such a vast amount that it will seem like it was nothing. We need to try to keep an eternal perspective.

Elder Donald L. Hallstrom said, "Recently, I was in a meeting with Elder Jeffrey R. Holland. In teaching the principle that mortal life can be agonizing but our hardships have eternal purpose—even if we do not understand it at the time—Elder Holland said, **'You can have what you want, or you can have something better**.'"[9] I love this thought. When we are passing through hard times, we must remember that, although we don't understand the "why" behind this trial, *God does*. And, if we continue forward, keeping the right attitude and holding firm to our faith, we will be blessed beyond measure for having done so.

9. Hallstrom, "Child of God," 27; emphasis added.

The Feelings of a First-Time Pregnant Mother

Satan has a way of even squeezing himself into great events and turning them against us if he can. Carolini Rocha (now Callis) was a remarkable sister missionary in our mission. Upon returning home from her mission and getting married in the temple, things were going great. When she first became pregnant, she and her husband were both very excited. But the following is something she shared with me during that first pregnancy and which she has given me permission to share. Perhaps some readers will be able to relate to her feelings:

> The enemy's whispers seem to be much stronger at certain times in our lives, and I am seeing this now at this time when I am going through my first pregnancy. Every day, I get a lot of negative thoughts that come to me: thoughts that I may not be able to educate, care for, and support my daughter, that she may not want to be my friend, that I may not be able to help her to know God in the best way. Every day thoughts come to me that my body will not be able to carry this pregnancy through to the end, that I am not strong enough to bring my daughter into this world. Every day I get thoughts that my body is ugly, my skin is ugly, I am not as attractive to my husband anymore because of the changes that have occurred so far with my body. Every day I need to struggle with these thoughts and the bad feelings that come with them. Praying in silence many times while crying has been the perfect refuge for that kind of feeling and there are days when I need to do this more than once.
>
> I know that God hears me pray because I just need to start saying, "Heavenly Father," and the thoughts and feelings start to be relieved. I know that the enemy tries to make us feel bad in the most fragile moments of life (like a pregnancy, for example), but I also know that in those same moments, the Lord can help us to be even stronger.

Recognize the Genesis of All Negative Thoughts

In those moments when negative thoughts from the adversary enter in, even if we at first mistakenly believe that they are our own thoughts, we need to remind ourselves of what we have been told in the scriptures. In Omni 1:25, we read, "There is nothing which is good save it comes from the Lord: and **that which is evil cometh from the devil**" (emphasis added). Alma 5:40 says, "For I say unto you that whatsoever is good cometh from God, and **whatsoever is evil cometh from the devil**" (emphasis added). Finally, to put an exclamation point on this teaching, in Moroni 7:12–14 (as we have shared previously), we are told, "Wherefore, all things which are good cometh of God; and **that which is evil cometh of the devil; for the devil is an enemy unto God, and fighteth against him continually, and inviteth and enticeth to sin, and to do that which is evil continually**. But behold, that which is of God inviteth and enticeth to do good continually; wherefore, every thing which inviteth and enticeth to do good, and to love God, and to serve him, is inspired of God. Wherefore, take heed, my beloved brethren, that ye **do not judge that which is evil to be of God**, or that which is good and of God to be of the devil" (emphasis added). In verse 17, the message continues: "For after this manner doth the devil work, for **he persuadeth no man to do good, no, not one**; neither do his angels; neither do they who subject themselves unto him" (emphasis added).

From these scriptures, we learn that, even if we think that a negative thought was our own thought, we can know with certainty that, at the core, any and **ALL NEGATIVE THOUGHTS ARE ACTUALLY FROM THE DEVIL!** Do not help his cause by continuing with those thoughts. Train yourself to push them out of your mind as soon as they come. I promise you that, if you will stay at it, you can train yourself to no longer accept any negative thoughts. And being successful at that will *change your life*!

The Feelings of Not Being Good Enough or Being Worthy

This next story happened many times on our mission, with many different missionaries. Of course, every story is somewhat different from the others, but they all have to do with the adversary working hard to make us feel that we are less than we are. He wants us to feel that we are not "enough" (not good enough, not worthy enough, and the like). I'm sure that, at one time or another, everyone has had it happen in their lives. It is such a common—and, unfortunately, such a *successful*—strategy of the adversary's that we need to expose it in order for us all to recognize it better when it happens to us in the future.

This story was shared with me by a wonderfully patient and loving sister missionary of ours, Sister Gleice de Jesus (now Lopes). She told me that one time, as soon as she was transferred to a new area, the adversary used that time of change as an opportunity to attack her. She said that as soon as she arrived in the area, she immediately was overcome by a heavy, negative spirit that seemed to almost literally *weigh on her* day and night. Interestingly, she noted that the area was a good area, and they had a good teaching group of people getting ready for baptism. Nevertheless, this negative feeling had such an impact on her that it actually made her feel physically weak. One night, she awoke to serious negative thoughts that invaded her mind. She even had a strong feeling that she had cancer and that this was why she was feeling weak. Since there was a history of cancer in her family, she was very scared. She got on her knees and prayed for help.

When the day dawned, Sister de Jesus's head was full of doubts. The adversary was speaking to her in the first person. She said that even though the thoughts were "you" instead of "I," she clearly felt that it was her saying these things to herself, literally "attacking herself." The thoughts included, "You're not prepared to do what needs to happen in this area," "You're not worthy to do the great work that needs to be done here," and "You don't deserve to even be by the side of this companion that you have." That whole morning, during her personal study, those nonstop thoughts consumed her. The last message that came to her, almost as an *exclamation point,* was, "You are too weak to do what you've been called to do here."

Sister de Jesus spent that entire day trying hard to push those negative thoughts out of her head. But the adversary doesn't give up easily. As he saw her working hard to rid herself of those feelings, he "doubled down" on her. As she and her companion were working that day, they came across a man who stopped them on the street. This man, obviously under the promptings of the adversary—whether he thought he was doing good or not—started repeating to her all of the same things that she had been thinking about herself all morning long. At first, Sister de Jesus was about to give up and totally give in to these thoughts. She felt that this man was confirming that what she had been telling herself all night and all morning must really be true!

Then, just when she was about to give up, the Holy Ghost took over. Her spirit seemed to wake up, and she bore a firm and strong testimony to this man by her authority as a representative of Jesus Christ. She also bore a powerful testimony of her Savior. As she did so, all of those terrible feelings immediately flew from her. She was overcome with an almost physical feeling of peace, warmth, and love. She knew in that moment that all of those previous thoughts and feelings were from the adversary because they left her when the Spirit began taking over. She told me that everything that had happened up until that point almost consumed and overcame her. The Spirit entered at her very lowest point. The Lord knew when it was just too much for her to take and confirmed for her that it had all been a lie from Satan.

These Feelings Don't Happen Only on Missions

Another wonderful sister missionary from our mission shared the following story with me. At her request, I have agreed to keep her story anonymous, but I hope it can help illustrate what Satan does to us:

> Shortly after coming home from my mission, I was living on my own in an apartment while I attended BYU. Also, at the time, I didn't know that I had some underlying health conditions

that affected my ability to stay awake while studying for school, studying my scriptures, and, yes, even praying. When I started having these problems, I heard many thoughts in my mind telling me that I was failing in my duty to Heavenly Father and not taking my scripture study and prayers seriously because I was falling asleep. I became extremely discouraged as I listened to those whisperings. As I tried to improve, and still found myself falling asleep frequently, those whisperings got stronger and more penetrating to my soul.

Pretty soon, I was hearing what I thought to be my own logic, telling me, "You can't feel the Spirit like you did on your mission because you lost it. You don't deserve the Spirit with you anymore. You'll never feel the Spirit like you did on your mission." I then began to doubt my ability to receive revelation or to learn anything new from the scriptures, regardless of my efforts. These thoughts became so frequent that I started to lose the desire to even try reading and praying. Then I started to struggle with even wanting to go to church. I felt that I was a lonely college student in a family ward. I told myself that I didn't seem to be feeling the Spirit when I attended church, anyway. So why go? I remember feeling that I was in a very dark place.

Fortunately, I had a wonderful bishop who checked on me regularly (it helped that he was also my neighbor). And he had given me an assignment to prepare a Sunday evening devotional for the young women on how to recognize the Spirit. It was in my preparation for that devotional that I truly felt the Spirit, Heavenly Father's love for me, and the push to just keep doing my best no matter what my best looked like. Then, as I did my best, I felt approval from the Spirit every time, until the whisperings of Satan faded away enough for me to finally be able to totally dismiss them.

One of the things I love the most about this story was how she had a loving bishop who must have been acting on a prompting (a *Bing!*) given to him to reach out to her and ask her to give that Sunday evening devotional. I am not even sure that he understood just how much of an impact it would have on her. However, because he acted on a small and simple prompting, he saved this wonderful young woman from a terrible path that the adversary was carefully trying to guide her down, which would have led to a terrible ending.

Yes, the adversary will continue to try to convince us to disregard the promptings from the Holy Ghost to say and do things that will bless the lives of others. He will attack our self-esteem and will talk to us in the first person and even get us to do his work for him by convincing us to take ownership of those negative thoughts. He is happy if he just gets us to take the next "downward step." His patience is amazing, knowing that, as we continue on that path—no matter how slowly—he will eventually destroy us. Unfortunately, many times, we don't even recognize that we are on that path.

Use a Full-Court Press

I am sure that some readers of this book may be asking how they can fight back against these negative promptings from the adversary. In basketball, some teams use a full-court press when they need to stop the other team from having as much success against them. In this situation, a team will defend their opponent for the entire length of the floor. This can cause their opponent to make many mistakes and fail in their offensive efforts. We need to do the same thing with the adversary when he tries to use negative self-talk with us. We should use a "full-court press" against him and his tactics. In order for a full-court press to be effective, it has to be put into place from the second the ball is brought in bounds. You don't have time to wait and decide to put it in place. And, in our fight to protect ourselves against Satan, we also don't have the luxury of being able to wait before we act, either. The acronym "PRESS" can help us remember how to fight back. Each letter refers to a tool we can use to stop Satan from hurting us:

P = **P**ray: This should always be the first thing we think of. When in doubt, we should stop, get on our knees, and talk to Heavenly Father.

R = **R**ead:	When negative thoughts come, turning to the scriptures can be a way to bring the Spirit back quickly.
E = **E**xact Opposite:	One tactic that has worked for me and some others is that when the adversary prompts me with negative thoughts about myself or to do something that is wrong, I choose to do, think, or say the exact opposite. I want him to know that, as he tries to influence me to do something wrong, he is actually going to help me to be better. If he sees that the results of his promptings actually help me to become even better, perhaps he will quit trying so hard.
S = **S**ing or Serve:	For some, singing a hymn will chase the negative thoughts from the adversary away. Or, for almost everyone, serving someone else is a magical way to feel much better! If you don't know someone you can serve, how about serving someone in need on the other side of the veil by doing work for them in the temple?
S = **S**upport System:	Who is your friend or relative that you can count on to always pump you up when you are feeling down? A quick call to that wonderful person may be just what you need. Don't ever be afraid to call for help (from God first, but also from one of your own "angels in disguise" here on earth).

It's not necessary to try to use all of these tools at one time to fight against the adversary. One of these tools will work best for one person and another will work better for a different person. But, in order for your "full-court press" to work, you need to decide beforehand which tool you feel will work best for you and be ready to call on it the instant that you feel the negative thoughts coming your way, recognizing that those thoughts are not yours but whispers from the enemy of your soul.

As we train ourselves to never accept any negative thoughts and to act on the whisperings of the first voice—those promptings from the Holy Ghost—we will be like those whom the Lord talks about in Doctrine and Covenants 59:23, when He says, "He who doeth the works of righteousness shall receive his reward, even peace in this world, and eternal life in the world to come." May it ever be so for each of us!

CHAPTER 6

Distraction: Another Favorite Tool of the Enemy

"The Spirit's voice is ever present, but it is calm. . . . The adversary tries to smother this voice with a multitude of loud, persistent, persuasive, and appealing voices."

—Elder James E. Faust[1]

In his October 2019 general conference talk, Elder Peter M. Johnson said, "You are elect sons and daughters of God. You have the power to overcome the adversary. The adversary, however, is aware of who you are. He knows of your divine heritage and seeks to limit your earthly and heavenly potential by using the three Ds: **Deception—Distraction—Discouragement**" (emphasis added).

As pointed out by Elder Johnson, the adversary uses these three key strategies to throw us off course. We already spoke a bit about the first D—deception—in chapter 4, as we discussed how Satan gets people to fall for the logic of the second voice. Then, in chapter 5, we discussed the third D—discouragement—as we warned about the negative self-talk that really is not self-talk at all, but actually promptings coming from him. In fact, in the case of the adversary's fake negative self-talk, he is using both discouragement *and* deception. Now, let's discuss the other D—distraction.

---

1. Faust, "Voice of the Spirit."

Satan knows that he cannot stop the Holy Ghost from fulfilling his role in giving us revelations, so he attacks where he knows he has a chance. He attacks *us*. He works hard to keep us from receiving these important promptings from the Holy Ghost. In this chapter, we will seek to better understand the adversary's strategy of distraction that keeps us from hearing and recognizing the Holy Ghost's promptings. We want to remove all barriers that keep us from receiving the communications that God is sending to us through the Holy Ghost.

President Nelson's optimism, coupled with his admonition, is clear. He said,

> **I am optimistic about the future**. It will be filled with opportunities for each of us to progress, contribute, and take the gospel to every corner of the earth. But I am also not naive about the days ahead. **We live in a world that is complex and increasingly contentious. The constant availability of social media and a 24-hour news cycle bombard us with relentless messages. If we are to have any hope of sifting through the myriad of voices and the philosophies of men that attack truth, we must learn to receive revelation**.[2]

Notice how he points out that all of these things that "bombard us" are making it much more difficult to hear God. It seems to me that he is telling us that we *must* make time for daily communication—*two-way communication*—with our Heavenly Father.

First Order of Business in a Military Invasion

In his 1991 general conference address, Elder Boyd K. Packer—speaking from experience after having served in World War II—gave us some valuable insight into a key strategy employed by the enemy to our souls:

> This trend to more noise, more excitement, more contention, less restraint, less dignity, less formality is not coincidental nor innocent nor harmless.

---

2. Nelson, "Revelation for Our Lives," 96; emphasis added.

> **The first order issued by a commander mounting a military invasion is the jamming of the channels of communication of those he intends to conquer.**
>
> **Irreverence suits the purposes of the adversary by obstructing the delicate channels of revelation in both mind and spirit.**[3]

Elder Packer's warning was given back in 1991. Many more "advancements" have been introduced since then that continue to jam our spiritual channels of communication.

A Message from the President of the Church

In the priesthood session of the April 2021 general conference, President Russell M. Nelson talked about the many lessons that the Lord wanted us to learn from the Covid-19 pandemic. He listed four specific ones, the fourth being, "We hear Jesus Christ better when we are still." Part of his counsel regarding this lesson included the following:

> We live in a time prophesied long ago, when "all things shall be in commotion; and surely, men's hearts shall fail them; for fear shall come upon all people" [Doctrine and Covenants 88:91]. That was true before the pandemic, and it will be true after. . . . In contrast, the voice of the Lord is not 'a voice of a great tumultuous noise, but . . . it [is] a still voice of perfect mildness, [like] a whisper, and it [pierces] even to the very soul' [Helaman 5:30]. *In order to hear this still voice, you too must be still!* [Psalm 46:10]
>
> For a time, the pandemic has canceled activities that would normally fill our lives. Soon we may be able to choose to fill that time again with the noise and commotion of the world. Or we can use our time to hear the voice of the Lord whispering His guidance, comfort, and peace. **Quiet time is**

3. Packer, "Reverence Invites Revelation," 22; emphasis added.

> **sacred time—time that will facilitate personal revelation and instill peace.**"[4]

Similarly, Elder Joseph B. Wirthlin admonished us, "I fear that some members of the Lord's Church 'live far beneath our privileges' with regard to the gift of the Holy Ghost. **Some are distracted by the things of the world that block out the influence of the Holy Ghost, preventing them from recognizing spiritual promptings. This is a noisy and busy world that we live in. Remember that being busy is not necessarily being spiritual. If we are not careful, the things of this world can crowd out the things of the Spirit."**[5]

Our "Spiritual War"

Let's assume for a minute that we are soldiers in a war and we are deep inside enemy territory. We know that the enemy could be coming our way at any time. We have the ammunition necessary to fight against them and win *as long as we know when and from where they are coming.* We have also been notified by our leaders that our side has satellites to see when and from where the enemy will be getting closer to us so that they can notify us where they are and how many of them there are. We have been informed that they will quietly speak to us on our communication devices when this happens. Each of us has our own communication device. But we are all spread out, individually. To get the message, we need to be carefully listening for the message to come.

Knowing that this is the case, how many of us would want to put our earbuds in and listen to our favorite songs rather than carefully pay attention to whatever kind of communication we will hear from our leaders? Spiritually speaking, that is what we are doing when we continually put our focus on the enticing "distractions" that Satan places before us instead of giving ourselves some important quiet time with God. It is obvious that we will have to use these things on a regular basis. But we should work to avoid allowing our lives to be taken

4. Nelson, "What We Are Learning," 80; emphasis added.
5. Wirthlin, "Unspeakable Gift," 27; emphasis added.

over by them. And we should work to find a time each day that is free from distractions and check our communication lines with heaven.

Being Online Can Take Us Offline with God

Elder Donald L. Hallstrom told us, "The more distractions that surround us, the easier it is to **treat casually, then ignore, and then forget** our connection with God."[6] That's the "regression" that Satan wants as he carefully leads us—step by step—away from God.

Elder Peter M. Johnson said,

> In our day, there are many distractions, including Twitter, Facebook, virtual reality games, and much more. These technological advances are amazing, but if we are not careful, they can distract us from fulfilling our divine potential. Using them appropriately can bring forth the power of heaven and allow us to witness miracles as we seek to gather scattered Israel on both sides of the veil. ***Let us be careful and not casual in our use of technology.*** Continually seek for ways that technology can draw us closer to the Savior and allow us to accomplish His work as we prepare for His Second Coming.[7]

Elder Stephen W. Owen shared a personal example from his life with which all of us can relate:

> Not long ago I woke up and prepared to study the scriptures. I picked up my smartphone and sat in a chair next to my bed with the intention of opening the Gospel Library app. I unlocked my phone and was just about to begin studying when I saw a half dozen notifications for text messages and emails that had come during the night. I thought, "I'll quickly check those messages, and then I'll get right to the scriptures." Well, two hours later I was still reading text messages, emails, news briefs, and social media posts. When I realized what

---

6. Hallstrom, "Child of God," 28; emphasis added.
7. Johnson, "Power to Overcome," 110; emphasis added.

time it was, I frantically rushed to get ready for the day. That morning I missed my scripture study, and consequently I didn't get the spiritual nourishment I was hoping for.[8]

How many times has this, or something equivalent to it, happened to you? This is Satan's goal with his "enticing distractions." Those things that Elder Owen was reading weren't bad things, but they were taking him away from what would have been much better.

It Will Take a Focused Effort

President Russell M. Nelson taught, "As we seek to be disciples of Jesus Christ, **our efforts to hear Him need to be ever more intentional**. It takes conscious and consistent effort to fill our daily lives with His words, His teachings, His truths. We simply cannot rely upon information we bump into on social media. **With billions of words online and in a marketing-saturated world constantly infiltrated by noisy, nefarious efforts of the adversary, where *can* we go to hear Him?**" In that same message, President Nelson then gave some ways that we can "hear Him":

1. Go to the scriptures.
2. Be in the temple.
3. Refine our ability to recognize the whisperings of the Holy Ghost.
4. Heed the words of the prophets, seers, and revelators.[9]

Regarding refining our ability to recognize the whisperings of the Holy Ghost, he said,

> **It has never been more imperative to know how the Spirit speaks to you than right now. In the Godhead, the Holy Ghost is the messenger. He will bring thoughts to your mind which the Father and Son want you to receive.** He is the Comforter. He will bring a feeling of peace to your heart. He testifies of truth and will confirm what is true as you hear

8. Owen, "Be Faithful, Not Faithless," 12.
9. Nelson, "Hear Him," 89–90; emphasis added.

> and read the word of the Lord. **I renew my plea for you to do *whatever* it takes to increase your spiritual capacity to receive personal revelation**. Doing so will help you know how to move ahead with your life, what to do during times of crisis, and how to discern and avoid the temptations and the deceptions of the adversary.[10]

Hearing God's Promptings above the Noise All around Us

In a great article in *LDS Living*, Dr. Taylor Halverson and Doug Witney shared a story that illustrates what we need to do in our daily lives:

> Back when the telegraph was the fastest method of long-distance communication, a young man applied for a job as a Morse Code operator. Answering an ad in the newspaper, he went to the office address that was listed. When he arrived, he entered a large, busy office filled with noise and clatter, including the sound of the telegraph in the background. A sign on the receptionist's counter instructed job applicants to fill out a form and wait until they were summoned to enter the inner office.
>
> The young man filled out his form and sat down with the seven other applicants in the waiting area. After a few minutes, the young man stood up, crossed the room to the door of the inner office, and walked right in. Naturally the other applicants perked up, wondering what was going on. They murmured among themselves that they hadn't heard any summons. They assumed the man who went into the office made a mistake and would be disqualified.
>
> Within a few minutes, however, the employer escorted the young man out of the office and said to the other applicants, "Gentlemen, thank you very much for coming, but the job has just been filled." The other applicants began grumbling to

10. Nelson, 90; emphasis added.

each other, and one spoke up saying, "Wait a minute, I don't understand. He was the last to come in, and we never got a chance to be interviewed. Yet he got the job. That's not fair!"

The employer said, "I'm sorry, but all the time you've been sitting here, the telegraph has been ticking out the following message in Morse Code, 'If you understand this message then come right in. The job is yours.' None of you heard it or understood it. This young man did. The job is his."[11]

This story is such a clear analogy of what happens in our daily lives. There is constant "noise and clatter" and other distractions around us at all times. That won't change. So the difference has to be *inside us.* What are we *tuned into hearing* above all the "noise and clatter"? It takes a consistent, focused effort, but if we stick with it, the rewards will be greater than we can ever imagine!

Elder David A. Bednar shared a story from his life that conveys the same important message in a slightly different way:

I once was traveling to a stake conference assignment on a small and noisy commuter airplane. Seated in the row just in front of me on the plane was a woman with three young children ranging in age from an infant to a four-year-old. Because the plane had only two seats on each side of the center aisle, the mother was situated quite some distance from her oldest child, a cute little boy who obviously was flying on an airplane for the very first time. His nose was pressed firmly against the window so he would have a good view of everything that was taking place, and he delighted in describing what he was seeing to his mother as the engines started and as we taxied down the runway for takeoff. The little boy's eyes were wide, and his voice was full of excitement as the plane climbed into the sky.

During all of this time, however, the mother was busy with the two youngest children, getting them buckled into their seats, finding toys, and responding to their needs and

11. Halverson and Witney, "2 Things Distracting Us."

> requests. The mother consistently had been responding to the little boy's enthusiastic exclamations in a calm, soothing voice. But because of the noise of the engines and the clatter of the small airplane, the little boy could not hear his mother's responses. After we had been in the air for about five minutes, and thinking that his mother was not paying adequate attention to him, the little boy blurted out, *"Mom, you're not listening to me!"*
>
> I then observed a very interesting thing. **The wise mother continued to respond and talk to her son in the same calm tones, never raising her voice**. Eventually the little boy was able to hear his mom's voice in spite of the engine and other noises on the plane. **The mother's voice did not change; rather, the little boy's ability to hear her voice in the midst of the noise increased.** It took some time, but the little boy learned how to block out the distracting noises around him and focus upon the familiar voice of his mother.
>
> Brothers and sisters, as we desire and invite the Holy Ghost into our lives and learn to heed simple promptings quickly, **we too can block out the distracting noises of the world and clearly focus upon the promptings of the Holy Ghost**.[12]

These distractions will be all around us during our entire lives. Satan will use all he can to knock us off track. But, as Julie B. Beck said, "Because personal revelation is a constantly renewable source of strength, **it is possible to feel bathed in help even during turbulent times**."[13] So it really isn't a question of whether the distractions will be there; **it is a *fact* that they will be**. Rather, the question is, to which source will we be tuned into and listening? What a great thought that, even during turbulent times in our lives—and we all have passed through them and will continue to do so—we can still feel "bathed in help."

---

12. Bednar, "Receiving, Recognizing, and Responding"; emphasis added.
13. Beck, "Upon the Handmaids, 11; emphasis added.

Like the little boy on the plane who couldn't hear his mother at first, the Nephites were faced with the same challenge as Christ was preparing to appear unto them. In 3 Nephi 11:3–6, we read,

> And it came to pass that while they were thus conversing one with another, they heard a voice as if it came out of heaven; and they cast their eyes round about, for **they understood not the voice which they heard**; and it was not a harsh voice, neither was it a loud voice; nevertheless, and notwithstanding it being a small voice it did pierce them that did hear to the center, insomuch that there was no part of their frame that it did not cause to quake; yea, it did pierce them to the very soul, and did cause their hearts to burn. **And it came to pass that again they heard the voice, and they understood it not. And again the third time they did hear the voice, and did open their ears to hear it; and their eyes were towards the sound thereof; and they did look steadfastly towards heaven, from whence the sound came. And behold, the third time they did understand the voice which they heard** (emphasis added).

As with these three great examples we just shared, we too can often hear a voice (God's voice) and not understand it until we focus on the voice and tune out other things.

Being Alive during Christ's Ministry

I'm sure many of us have read certain scriptures and felt that we would never be like the people in that scripture. For example, with the story of Moses and the children of Israel who were bitten by the fiery serpents, I remember feeling, "Come on! If I was dying and Moses said that all I needed to do in order to live was to look at the brass serpent, I would have at least turned my head to look. What would I have to lose?" Yet we do not know for sure how we would have reacted.

The example that is perhaps most illustrative is all of the people who interacted with the Savior of the world during His mortal ministry. They were in the daily presence of Jesus Christ, the Savior of all mankind. He would pay the price of sin for all of humanity. And yet most people who interacted with Him didn't view Him for who He was. This is absolutely the most perfect example of how the adversary is able to distract people. The Savior was among them, but they saw a carpenter's son. Their focus was on the wrong things, and thus they were not able to hear what the Spirit was trying to tell them.

To a lesser degree—but just as important in their lives—this is what happens to many people that the missionaries teach and try to prepare for baptism. They hear the discussions and may even feel something as the missionaries begin teaching them. Some even set a date for baptism. But then something happens. The "distractions" from the adversary enter into the equation. In some cases, he gets them to put off the next discussion for such a long period of time that they begin to forget what they had felt. Then they decide that they have other priorities and cancel the appointments with the missionaries.

In other cases, Satan will put family or friends in their path who will say negative things about the Church—vocalizing the thoughts he puts into their heads—and get them to question what they had felt. The peer pressure alone may get them to cancel future appointments. In yet other cases, he will help them find things on the internet that will put doubts in their minds. Soon, what once was an exciting path of someone coming unto Christ turns into just one more win for the adversary, all because of the distractions that took their focus off of what they felt from the Holy Ghost as the missionaries taught them.

Our Own Feelings Can Be the Distraction the Enemy Uses

Thus far, we have talked about the distractions of the world that the enemy uses to keep us from receiving communication from the Holy Ghost. However, we can also do this to ourselves by the choices we make. Besides the decision to "plug into" all of the technological distractions that we have discussed, we can chase the Spirit away by other means as well. For example, we can also be distracted because of those with whom we choose to associate. If our friends choose to do things or say things that drive the Spirit away, and we choose to stay in their association, we put ourselves outside of the Spirit's reach.

Another concern is what our own emotions can do. Elder Richard G. Scott warned us that we can keep ourselves from feeling the promptings of the Spirit. He spoke of something that perhaps we may not consider to be an impediment to our ability to hear the Spirit: our own emotions. He said, "The inspiring influence of the Holy Spirit can be overcome or masked by strong emotions, such as anger, hate, passion, fear, or pride. When such influences are present, it is like trying to savor the delicate flavor of a grape while eating a jalapeño pepper. Both flavors are present, but one completely overpowers the other. In like manner, strong emotions overcome the delicate promptings of the Holy Spirit."[14] This is an important warning for us all to consider.

Elder Stephen W. Owen said, "The adversary will try to persuade you that spiritual nourishment isn't necessary or, more cunningly, that it can wait. **He is the master of distraction and author of procrastination. He will bring things to your attention that seem urgent but in reality aren't that important. He would have you become so 'troubled about many things' that you neglect the 'one thing [that] is needful'** [Luke 10:41–42]."[15]

Elder Dallin H. Oaks said, "Team sports and technology toys like video games and the Internet are already winning away the time of our children and youth. Surfing the Internet is not better than serving the Lord or strengthening the family. . . . **Some young people are amusing themselves to death—spiritual death**."[16]

President Ezra Taft Benson taught,

> **Take time to meditate**. Meditation on a passage of scripture—James 1:5—led a young boy into a grove of trees to commune with his Heavenly Father. That is what opened the heavens in this dispensation.
>
> Meditation on a passage of scripture from the book of John in the New Testament brought forth the great revelation on the three degrees of glory.

---

14. Scott, "To Acquire Spiritual Guidance," 8.
15. Owen, 13; emphasis added.
16. Oaks, 107; emphasis added.

> Meditation on another passage of scripture from the Epistle of Peter opened the heavens to President Joseph F. Smith, and he saw the spirit world. That revelation, known as the Vision of the Redemption of the Dead, is now a part of the Doctrine and Covenants.[17]

President Benson's message is clear. Although we have natural distractions that we must participate in—with work and other necessary activities—he points out that **we *must* find time to meditate and be free from distractions**. That is when the Lord can talk to us, just as we heard earlier from the Prophet Joseph.

Sister Michelle D. Craig—serving at the time as the first counselor in the Young Women General Presidency—said something similar in her October 2019 general conference address:

> **As you use your agency to carve out time every day to draw close to God's voice, especially in the Book of Mormon, over time His voice will become clearer and more familiar to you**. In contrast, the *distractions* and *noise* that fill the world and our homes and our lives can make it more difficult to hear His voice. These distractions can so occupy our minds and hearts that we leave no room for the gentle promptings of the Holy Ghost. . . .
>
> Satan wants to separate us from God's voice by keeping us out of those quiet places. If God speaks in a still, small voice, you and I need to draw close to hear Him. Just imagine what would happen if we were as intent on staying connected with heaven as we are on staying connected to Wi-Fi! **Pick a time and place, and listen for God's voice every day. And keep this sacred appointment with exactness, for so very much depends on it!**[18]

I pray that we will daily pick a time and place to make time for God. It will quickly become our favorite part of each day!

---

17. Benson, "Seek the Spirit," 2; emphasis added.
18. Craig, "Spiritual Capacity," 19; emphasis added.

SECTION THREE

The Adventure Begins!

CHAPTER 7

Procrastination: Satan's Plan B

"We watch. We wait. We listen for that still, small voice. When it speaks, wise men and women obey. We do not postpone following promptings of the Spirit."

—Elder Thomas S. Monson[1]

Now that we have spent time understanding how to recognize the promptings of the adversary, let's return our focus to those important promptings of the Holy Ghost. It is critical that we learn to not only recognize and act on the promptings of the Holy Ghost but that we also commit to always *act on those promptings as soon as they come to us.* You never know when a prompting you are getting is "mission critical" and very time sensitive in the life of the person you are prompted to help. Because of this, it is always best to make it your habit to act right away. That way, you will never have to worry about whether you responded in time or not.

Michelle D. Craig said, "***Act without delay***. When you receive promptings and then act with intention, the Lord can use you. The more you act, the more familiar the voice of the Spirit becomes. You will increasingly recognize God's guidance and that He is 'willing . . . to reveal His mind and will.' ***If you delay, you might forget the prompting or miss the chance to help someone for God.***"[2]

1. Monson, "Spirit Giveth Life," 68.
2. Craig, "Spiritual Capacity," 19; emphasis added.

When Plan A Doesn't Work, Satan Goes to Plan B

First and foremost, the adversary works to get us to agree with his logic to not act on a prompting that came from the Holy Ghost. However, when he sees that he won't have success going that route, he immediately switches to his extremely effective plan B, which is to agree with us that it is important to do that thing but to get us to put it off for a bit and do it later. We need to recognize that this is a very dangerous and slippery slope he is leading us down. ***Procrastination is one of the adversary's greatest tools***. Sometimes, that will be all he needs to do because, by not acting immediately, we will miss the chance to bless the life of that other person. Other times, by procrastinating now, we will end up forgetting about it altogether and never do it at all.

Elder Ronald A. Rasband shared the following from his personal experience: "I distinctly recall a time when I received a prompting in answer to mighty prayer. The answer was clear and powerful. However, **I failed to act immediately on the prompting, and after a period of time I began to wonder if what I had felt had been real**. Some of you may have fallen for that deception of the adversary as well."[3] We have probably all had similar experiences. You can see the genius of Satan in using this strategy with us.

Joseph Smith instituted a rule in his life to combat ever having such feelings come to him. He said, "**I made this my rule: When the Lord commands, do it**."[4]

Elder Gene R. Cook said that Satan uses different strategies with members than he does with non-members, but with the goal of reaching the same results: "He teaches the world not to pray, but to the Saints he simply says, 'Don't pray now. You don't feel like praying right now' (see 2 Nephi 32:8-9). **The net effect is the same**."[5] This is a startling statement on how Satan knows that getting us to procrastinate doing the right thing can be just as effective as getting us to commit to not do it at all.

---

3. Rasband, "Lest Thou Forget," 115; emphasis added.
4. Smith, Joseph, *History of the Church*, 2:170; emphasis added.
5. Cook, "Spiritual Guides," 25; emphasis added.

The Song That Was Never Sung

Marion G. Romney shared a short story that haunted him for a very long time:

> I remember another occasion when I was in Australia on a mission. I went up to visit the Jenolan Caves—very wonderful, spectacular caves. And as we walked through them, the guide said, "If some of you will get out and stand on that rock over there and sing a song, it will demonstrate the capacity of this cave."
>
> Well, the Spirit said to me, "Go over there and sing 'O, My Father.'" I hesitated, and the crowd walked on. I lost the opportunity. I never felt good about that. The only thing that ever made me feel the Lord had forgiven me was when I heard President McKay say, "I was inspired one time to do a certain thing when I was in the mission field, and I didn't do it." He said, "I have always been sorry since." He said, "**Never fail to respond to the whisperings of the Spirit. Live so you can receive it, and then have the courage to do as it instructs**."[6]

The Letters That Were Never Mailed

Elder Cledson Santos was already a great missionary and leader in our mission when I arrived as the new mission president. He was a very impressive missionary who did a lot of wonderful work during his time in the mission field. He shared a story about his regret for putting off acting on the Spirit, but it also shows a glimpse of the kind of missionary that he was in the first place—always going above and beyond in his efforts to help and bless the lives of others. Here is his story in his own words:

> One day, when we went to lunch at a member's home, the lunch was not yet ready. Rather than waste any time just sitting and waiting, we left to make some contacts until lunch was ready

6. Romney, "Men of Courage," 74; emphasis added.

[Author's note: This is the kind of missionary that he was—never wanting to waste a minute of the Lord's time.] As soon as we left the home, we saw a lady on the other side of the street, standing behind a lamppost, attempting to hide from the scorching hot sun. Next to her were many heavy bags that she had been carrying. My companion and I went over to her and offered to help carry her bags the rest of the way to her home. She appeared a little nervous, but the heat and her exhaustion overcame her nervousness and she accepted our offer.

When we arrived at her house, she offered us water and we gladly accepted. Then, as she began thanking us for our help, out came a beautiful little girl, calling her "Grandmother." I asked about her. The woman said that she lived with her daughter and her granddaughter. The granddaughter was only five years old and her mother, Edna—another daughter of the woman we helped—was in prison for getting involved in the region's drug trafficking. I was moved by the situation. She told us that Edna had not seen her little five-year-old daughter since she was a baby. That really touched my heart. I asked the lady if she ever visited her daughter in prison. She said that she never had. The next time that we visited her, I felt impressed to ask her for Edna's prison mailing address and she gave it to me.

We kept going back and teaching this woman the gospel. We would meet with her every day at the same time. She was very firm in her evangelical beliefs, but she loved our visits and the things we were teaching her. I ended up writing a letter to her daughter, telling her that I had met her mother and her little daughter and that she should be proud because she was so beautiful. I tried to describe everything I saw, and everyone that was living with that family. Just two weeks later, I got a letter from Edna. She thanked me profusely for writing to her. She said that it was so awesome for her to hear things about her little angel. She said that neither her mother, nor anyone else, ever visited her or wrote letters to her. During all of the years that she had been in prison, I was the first person to write to her. She let me know that she wasn't sure if she would be able to write again if I wrote to her because she didn't have letters, papers, stamps or anything like that . . . and no money to purchase them.

On the next preparation day, I wrote to her again, and I included some papers, envelopes, and stamps so that she could write back. I also shared more details about her daughter. Finally, I decided to also write her about the gospel. She had said that she didn't have access to a Bible, so I wrote down some scripture verses for her. I taught about the Book of Mormon, faith, repentance, and baptism, among other gospel doctrines each week. Her mother, on the other hand, began to get a lot of opposition from the pastors at her church, who told her how dangerous we were and many other lies about our church. These comments really confused her, because she loved how she had been feeling with our lessons, but she trusted her pastors. This made her hold off on her previous decision to get baptized. After a few weeks, Edna wrote to her mother, but she let me know that she never got any response from her mom.

Unfortunately, soon thereafter, I was transferred from that area and given more leadership responsibilities within the mission. I began to have much less free time—even on my P-days. My transfer also took me to an area where the post office was far from where we lived. I still wrote to Edna every week, and I received letters from her from time to time. But, with my difficulties in not having much free time, even though I was writing to her, I would only mail the letters when I would think ahead of time that we would be passing by a post office so that I could send them. After a while, even writing letters to her became less frequent. With my added responsibilities and how tired it was making me, I stopped writing. Every week, I would still hear a voice reminding me to write Edna. Little by little, however, with each passing week that I would not write to her, that voice would get quieter and weaker until I could feel it less and less.

A few more months passed, and I was transferred to become the zone leader of the zone that had my old area in it—the area that had Edna's mom's house. One day, as I was doing a division with one of the missionaries who served in that area, I felt a very strong desire to go back and see Edna's mom, who I hadn't seen in a number of months. So we went.

When we arrived at her house, I was happy to be back at that same door where I had previously been excitedly greeted so many times by that beautiful little girl. When Edna's mom came to the gate, I gave her a big smile and let her know how glad I was to see her. But the poor woman looked kind of beaten. We talked a little and then I asked her about Edna. I was excited to hear how she was doing, because in the letters that I had exchanged with her in prison, she had been making progress. She was reading the verses from the Book of Mormon that I was sending her. She had been praying and repenting. It had been so long that I had not had any news about her that I was anxious to hear of her progress. Her mother then told me that, just seven days earlier, she had buried her daughter. *Edna had committed suicide in prison.* My smile vanished and my heart sank. I had to fight hard to keep from crying and collapsing right there in front of that woman and her granddaughter. For the rest of that day, I felt suffocated and devastated. I felt an agonizing pain.

When I got back to my apartment that night, I opened my suitcase and there were all the letters that I had written to Edna, *but that I had never found time to mail.* I cried that night and still, to this day, I am overcome with emotion every time I think about it. I carried those letters for a long time on the mission, *as a reminder that the voice of the Spirit always needs to be heard and followed immediately,* as lives depend on it.

I don't know if those letters would have prevented Edna from taking her own life, but they would have given her a little bit more strength and a little bit of joy in that place that had so little joy to offer. They could have been a light amidst the extreme darkness in which she found herself. Never had that quote from Joseph Smith touched me so deeply: "*When the Lord commands, do it!*" I learned a lot from this experience. I will never again put off acting on a prompting from the Spirit. I never want to feel that way again regarding anyone else (emphasis added).

My heart hurts every time I think of this experience from my beloved Elder C. Santos. It hurts me to know that this amazing missionary and servant of God will carry that hurt with him for the rest of his life. Yet, what he doesn't stop to think about—that I am proud of every time I think of this story—is what kind of a man and missionary he was to ask for Edna's prison address and to start writing her in the first place. He probably doesn't allow himself to stop and appreciate the joy that he brought to Edna with the many letters that she did get from him during those darkest days of her life. That is the kind of great man and missionary that he always was. But the story also serves as an important reminder for us to *never* put off a prompting! I hope that he—and others who have a similar story from their lives that haunts them about not acting immediately on a prompting—may be somewhat comforted to know that this has happened even to prophets of God. We read the story from Elder Romney and how he said that President McKay said it happened to him. Later in this chapter you will read a powerful story from President Monson's life as well.

You Can Be Prompted to Not Do Something You Want to Do

Most of the time in our lives, the promptings we will receive from the Holy Ghost will be to do something or say something that the Lord wants us to do or say. Less common—but just as important promptings to heed—will be the times when you may have an idea to say or do something, and the Holy Ghost will prompt you to *not* do or say that thing.

Such was the case with Robert L. Millet in a story that he shared in his book *The Holy Spirit*:

> A small group of students approached me and requested that I teach an Old Testament class. I really did not know a great deal about the Old Testament, given that I had only taught it once and that was to a rowdy but wonderful group of seminary students four years earlier in the Salt Lake Valley. I agreed to teach the institute class. The young people then asked, "Could

we do it at 6:00 a.m., so that we can get to our university classes on time?"

I smiled, gulped, and haltingly replied, "Sure. That would be fine." At least the institute class would not conflict with other classes!

We began the next week, and I found myself actually enjoying my study of the Old Testament. I managed to stay about two class periods ahead of the students. One morning we were moving along fairly well when a young woman raised her hand and posed a question about a potentially sensitive matter. I pondered for a moment to decide how to answer. One option was that I could provide a brief but accurate answer that wouldn't lead us into strange territory. Unfortunately, I had done a great deal of reading on this odd and tangential subject in recent months and realized that I could really impress the students with my extensive knowledge. **At that moment, the Spirit of the Lord very clearly prompted me to choose the former option and proceed with the remainder of the lesson.** I thought to myself, "But I really do know quite a bit about this matter." **The prompting came again, as though the Lord was speaking to me very directly: "Provide an adequate answer for now. That is all you need to do."**

Regrettably, I decided to set aside those two very clear warnings. Within ten minutes the room was filled with a spirit of unrest, and confusion began to spread. And, more practically, we wasted a great deal of time that could have been spent on more meaningful matters. The look on the faces of those young adults bespoke both discomfort and disappointment. I did my best to patch things up before the class was over. Finally everyone left the room, and I was left to reflect painfully on what had just taken place. **I had ignored the Holy Spirit's effort to keep me from a worthless exercise. I had turned a deaf ear to the voice of that member of the Godhead whose influence and comfort I had, ironically, sought for most earnestly for so many years**. My refusal to obey resulted in my quenching the Spirit, driving it out of our midst and leaving each one of us in a stupor of thought. It was an awful experience, one I have never forgotten.

Over the years since then, as I have studied the Book of Mormon, I have read with much interest and equal amount of regret of an encounter that took place some eighty years before Christ's birth. Alma's missionary companion Amulek was teaching the wicked people of Ammonihah when he was confronted by Zeezrom. "Will ye answer the questions which I shall put unto you?" inquired the crafty lawyer. Then came a timeless and treasured reply, one that I wish I had remembered before my debacle in institute class. "And Amulek said unto him: Yea, if it be according to the Spirit of the Lord, which is in me; **for I shall say nothing which is contrary to the Spirit of the Lord**" (Alma 11:21–22).[7]

If We Don't Act Now, We May Not Get the Chance to Act Later

Elder David A. Bednar asked the following question: "Have you ever received and recognized a prompting from the Holy Ghost, and then decided to respond to it '*later*'? And then when later arrived, you found that you could not remember the prompting. I have learned that acting upon promptings quickly greatly increases our capacity to receive and recognize the influence of the Holy Ghost."[8]

I know that, if we are totally honest, we would each respond that this has happened to us at some point in our lives. Perhaps it was a prompting that happened during a television program you were watching—like the example we gave earlier in this book—and you said, "I will when this show is over." But after the show was over you didn't even give it a second thought. Or perhaps it was late at night. You were tired and ready to go to bed and you got a prompting that you should send an email or give someone a call. At the time, you either decided that you were too tired and you would do it tomorrow (but, when tomorrow came, you forgot all about it), or you got

7. Millet, *Holy Spirit*, 94–95; emphasis added.
8. Bednar, "Receiving, Recognizing, and Responding."

another thought that said, "It's too late at night to call that person right now. I'll call tomorrow." What we didn't take into consideration is that *the Holy Ghost knew it was late and yet He still prompted you to make the call.*

Don't be afraid to follow your promptings. Just do it!

The Promise That Was Not Kept

Elder Andrey Eugênio was a great missionary in our mission who worked hard to follow the promptings of the Spirit. He shared an experience with me that probably has happened to many missionaries and to other members of the Church. Nonetheless, it serves as a great reminder for each of us. Here is his story in his own words:

> This happened in just my second transfer of my mission. My companion and I looked through the area book for people who had already been taught but had not accepted the gospel yet. We chose some names and went out to try to find these people. When we arrived at one house, we were greeted by a woman who said that she had just recently moved into that house—the person we were looking for did not live there anymore. We asked if she would like to hear our message, and she accepted.
>
> As we got into the message a little bit with her, it was evident that she really needed what we had to share with her. She shared with us that she had been going through a lot of difficulties in her life and that she had even recently thought about killing herself. We began teaching her. We would leave challenges for her—reading and praying—and she fulfilled each one of them. She went to church and accepted our invitation to prepare for baptism. We spent a few weeks teaching and preparing her, during which time, everything went perfectly. Then, during the week of her baptism, we had some meetings that we had to attend—zone conferences and other meetings. As a result, we had limited time to get things done in our area. For three days, we felt that we should go over to her house, but we made excuses for not following the Spirit and saying it was okay. Looking back now, it is obvious to see

that those excuses were the promptings of that second voice that our mission president had taught us about. Unfortunately, we didn't recognize this at the time and, since his logic made a lot of sense, we ended up following his promptings.

On Friday, we decided that we *had to find a way* to get to her house. When we got there, she wasn't there. We already felt that something had gone wrong with her baptism. The next day—Saturday—before lunch, we decided to go to her house again. She took a long time to answer the door but finally did. We sat down with her and asked about her baptism and if everything was all right. She said that it wasn't. She had been drinking and smoking almost all week. We began to tell her how she knew that it was wrong and that she had already promised us and God that she would not be doing those things anymore. That was when she told us a phrase that will haunt me for my whole life. She said: "I know what I did was wrong, but when you invited me to be baptized, you promised that you would stay with me and help me every day. **You said that you would be my 'spiritual protectors.' Then you just abandoned me. So, since you, as representatives of Christ, broke your promise to me, I felt that it was okay for me to break my promise to you**."

When she said that, the Spirit whispered in my ear: "All week long, I have been telling you to come, but you decided not to listen to me. Now, you *must* help her." We talked with her further. We apologized for what we had failed to do and explained about our meetings. But we recommitted to help her. She accepted our apology and agreed to continue to prepare for baptism in the next few weeks.

Just a few short minutes after we left her house, President Dalton called and told my companion and me that we were both being transferred immediately. I never did hear any more about her. I don't know if the missionaries that took over continued with her or not or if she was ever baptized. As a result, to this day, I am bothered by the fact that, if I had listened to the Spirit and gone to her house at the beginning of that week, her whole life would have been changed for the better. I have asked God many times to forgive me for not acting on those promptings. **I**

> **believe that I will never forget this experience. I failed that woman and I let the Spirit down, too.** But, if it was going to happen on my mission, I am glad it happened very early on. Because after that experience, I was committed for the rest of my mission—and since my mission ended, as well—to always not only obey the promptings of the Holy Ghost, but to do so immediately. I never again want to have the feeling that I had when I heard her say those words to us! (emphasis added).

The Important Lesson President Monson Learned the Hard Way

Soon after Thomas S. Monson was called to be a counselor in the First Presidency of the Church, Elder Jeffrey R. Holland wrote an article about him in the February 1986 *Ensign,* titled "President Thomas S. Monson: Man of Action, Man of Faith, Always 'on the Lord's Errand.'" In that wonderful article, he shared the following story from the life of President Monson:

> Twenty-three-year-old Tom Monson, relatively new bishop of the Sixth-Seventh Ward in the Temple View Stake, was uncharacteristically restless as the stake priesthood leadership meeting progressed. He had the distinct impression that he should leave the meeting immediately and drive to the Veterans' Hospital high up on the Avenues of Salt Lake City. Before leaving home that night he had received a telephone call informing him that an older member of his ward was ill and had been admitted to the hospital for care. Could the bishop, the caller wondered, find a moment to go by the hospital sometime and give a blessing? The busy young leader explained that he was just on his way to a stake meeting but that he certainly would be pleased to go by the hospital as soon as the meeting was concluded.
>
> Now the prompting was stronger than ever: "Leave the meeting and proceed to the hospital at once." But the stake president himself was speaking at the pulpit! It would be most discourteous to stand in the middle of the presiding officer's

message, make one's way over an entire row of brethren, and then exit the building altogether. Painfully he waited out the final moments of the stake president's message, then bolted for the door even before the benediction had been pronounced.

Running the full length of the corridor on the fourth floor of the hospital, the young bishop saw a flurry of activity outside the designated room. A nurse stopped him and said, "Are you Bishop Monson?"

"Yes," was his anxious reply.

"I'm sorry," she said. "The patient was calling your name just before he passed away."

Fighting back the tears, Thomas S. Monson turned and walked back into the night. **He vowed then and there that he would never again fail to act upon a prompting from the Lord**. He would acknowledge the impressions of the Spirit when they came, and he would follow wherever they led him, ever to be "on the Lord's errand."[9]

When I think of the best examples of people who immediately act on the promptings that the Spirit gives them, I would be hard-pressed to ever come up with a better example of someone that I have seen in my lifetime than President Monson. I have heard story after story of him following promptings and brightening the day of someone or changing people's lives. Yet even he had a moment that he regrets. In his case, he wasn't just doing something "good" at the time. I would argue that he was doing something "better" than "good." He was at a church priesthood leadership meeting, and he was absolutely right that it would have been "bad form" to get up and disrupt the entire meeting by leaving in the middle of his priesthood leader's talk. *But the Spirit knew that, too, and still urged him to get up and leave the meeting.* He learned from that experience and committed that he would never again choose the "good" or the "better" at the expense of doing what was "best." And that helped turn him into the President Monson that we all loved and admired so much.

9. Holland, "President Thomas S. Monson."

All of us should feel a little "less terrible" after reading the many stories we have shared of Apostles who, at some earlier point earlier in their lives, failed to act on a prompting, as well (such as Elder Romney, President McKay, and President Monson). So, if we haven't been perfect in this regard ourselves, we can stop beating ourselves up and, instead, do what these great men did. They vowed that it would never happen again!

I shared this quote previously, but it is applicable here as well. Elder Ronald A. Rasband said, "We must act on the *first* prompting. . . . **We must be confident in our first promptings**. Sometimes, we rationalize; we wonder if we are feeling a spiritual impression or if it is just our own thoughts. When we begin to second-guess, even third-guess, our feelings—and we all have—**we are dismissing the Spirit**; we are questioning divine counsel."[10]

He also said, "**First promptings are pure inspiration from heaven**. When they confirm or testify to us, we need to recognize them for what they are and never let them slip past. So often, **it is the Spirit inspiring us to reach out to someone in need**, family and friends in particular."[11]

This message from Elder Rasband was the lesson that Bishop Monson, Elder C. Santos, Elder Eugênio, and so many of us have learned the hard way. It is my prayer that the reader can learn from their stories instead of having to learn on your own later on in your life.

In our efforts to receive and act on these divine promptings, we would do well to heed the following counsel from Elder David A. Bednar:

> **I have learned that acting upon promptings quickly greatly increases our capacity to receive and recognize the influence of the Holy Ghost**. I have also learned that properly recording spiritual impressions demonstrates to the Savior how much I treasure His direction. The simple practice of writing down spiritual thoughts and feelings greatly enhances the likelihood of receiving and recognizing additional promptings from the Holy Ghost. . . . If you and I have a sincere desire

10. Rasband, "Holy Spirit Guide," 95–96; emphasis added.
11. Rasband, 96; emphasis added.

> for the constant companionship of the Holy Ghost, invite His influence into our lives through our obedience and actions, and learn to heed simple promptings and to do so quickly, then I testify and promise that **we will be able to tell the difference between our own emotions telling us what we want to hear and the Holy Ghost telling us what we need to hear**.[12]

What Happened after President Monson Learned His Lesson?

It is one thing to *say* that we have learned a lesson, but it's quite another when we *show* that we have learned our lesson through our future actions. Other than the difficult story we just shared from President Monson's life, in every other story I have heard about his experiences with the promptings from the Holy Ghost, he has shown that he learned that early lesson very well. Allow me to share one of my favorite stories from his life. President Monson shared this same story in two different general conference addresses, first in the April 1985 general conference and then again nearly thirty years later in the October 2012 general conference. I will quote the story as he told it in the latter conference talk:

> **I have learned, as I have mentioned in previous messages, never to postpone a prompting**. On one occasion many years ago, I was swimming laps at the old Deseret Gym in Salt Lake City when I felt the inspiration to go to the University Hospital to visit a good friend of mine who had lost the use of his lower limbs because of a malignancy and the surgery which followed. ***I immediately left the pool***, dressed, and was soon on my way to see this good man.
>
> When I arrived at his room, I found that it was empty. Upon inquiry I learned I would probably find him in the swimming pool area of the hospital, an area which was used for physical therapy. Such turned out to be the case. He had guided himself there in his wheelchair and was the only occupant of the room.

12. Bednar, "Receiving, Recognizing, and Responding"; emphasis added.

> He was on the far side of the pool, near the deep end. I called to him, and he maneuvered his wheelchair over to greet me. We had an enjoyable visit, and I accompanied him back to his hospital room, where I gave him a blessing.
>
> I learned later from my friend that he had been utterly despondent that day and **had been contemplating taking his own life**. He had prayed for relief but began to feel that his prayers had gone unanswered. He went to the pool with the thought that this would be a way to end his misery—by guiding his wheelchair into the deep end of the pool. **I had arrived at a critical moment, in response to what I know was inspiration from on high**.
>
> My friend was able to live many more years—years filled with happiness and gratitude. **How pleased I am to have been an instrument in the Lord's hands on that critical day at the swimming pool.**[13]

In most situations, we will not know if that particular prompting from the Holy Ghost is time sensitive or not. For that very reason, ***we should always assume that it is.*** Notice that President Monson did not even finish his swimming exercises for the day. Once he got that prompting, he said that he *immediately left the pool* and was on his way to see his friend. What would have been the result, had he decided to go see his friend *after he had finished swimming his laps*? It would have been too late!

It is not enough to act on the promptings of the Holy Ghost. We must commit ourselves to act *immediately* on every prompting. By so doing, we won't have to live with the regrets of failing to help someone by acting too late or by not acting at all.

Let's commit to be quick to respond to every prompting. We will *love* being the answer to the prayers of others. As President Thomas S. Monson said, "**Do not postpone a prompting; rather, act on it, and the Lord will open the way.**"[14]

---

13. Monson, "Consider the Blessings," 87; emphasis added.
14. Monson, "Sacred Call of Service," 55; emphasis added.

CHAPTER 8

We Don't Always Get to See How the Story Ends

"Often the timing is inconvenient, and we seldom know the impact of our small acts of service. But every now and then, we will recognize that we have been instruments in the hands of God and we will be grateful to know that the Holy Ghost working through us is a manifestation of God's approval."

—Michelle D. Craig[1]

They Are Not All "Happy Endings"

After I had taught my missionaries to believe the principle that a positive thought to say something or do something is a prompting from God and that we just need to have the conviction to act on every good prompting that comes to us regardless of the second voice that would follow it, many missionaries still expressed concern about being unable to tell the difference between a prompting from God and his or her own thought.

When I would ask what they meant, they would typically give me an example, such as a time when they had been walking down the street and felt like they had a prompting to do something—talk

1. Craig, "Divine Discontent," 54.

to someone on the street, clap at a home, or something similar. However, when they acted on the prompting, it turned out badly. For example, if they clapped at the home, either nobody answered the door or, if someone did answer, they were extremely rude to the missionaries. Similar results were shared about what happened with their promptings to stop and talk to someone on the street. They were convinced that, because it "didn't work out," it was proof that what they had felt couldn't have really been a prompting from the Holy Ghost.

Time after time, I tried to help my missionaries understand that following promptings of the Holy Ghost *doesn't come with a guarantee* that people will respond well. I would plead with them, **"Don't ever doubt your promptings!"**

I tried to teach my missionaries that as we act on promptings the Holy Ghost gives us, we need to realize something very important: *If it doesn't work out as we had expected that it would, that does not mean that it wasn't a prompting!* Many times, the Holy Ghost will prompt us to do something and, as we do it, it *won't* end in the perfect way—with the figurative nice little bow on it—as we hoped it would. Just because we did what God wanted us to do does not mean that the other person will respond to us in the way that we think he or she should. Why is this the case? It's because those people that we are prompted to reach out to still have their agency to choose how they will respond to us. However, that does not change the fact that *God indeed wanted* us to stop and talk to that person (or whatever it was that we were prompted to do).

I told our missionaries that we should never say, "I guess that wasn't really a prompting!" or "I guess it was just my own thought." That is what Satan wants you to believe. If he can get you to doubt your promptings, he knows that it is much more likely that you will quit acting on them in the future. We should not even say, "That didn't work out!" Instead, we should say something like this: "Hmm . . . that didn't work out the way I thought it would." Do you understand the difference? When we say, "That didn't work out," we are always wrong, because it is *never* a surprise to God! When He prompts us to do something, He already knows exactly how the person will respond to us acting on that prompting. When the person treats us rudely, He knew that would happen. However, He still wants to give that person the opportunity that we are giving him or her. God will never say, "Well, I'll be! That's a shocker!" He knows exactly how people will respond. So it's okay to think that it didn't work out the way *that you expected it would,* but you should never think that *it didn't work out.*

I'll repeat this point one more time because it is so important: *Just because it didn't turn out the way that you had expected or hoped it would does **not** mean that it wasn't a prompting from God!* I almost want to suggest that you repeat this again at least ten times. It is so important to remember, but my experience has been that—even after people learn this principle—it is easily forgotten the next time that they act and don't see an obvious "happily ever after" ending.

The attitude that we all need to have is this: When you act on promptings from the Holy Ghost, ***it always works out.*** If you act on a prompting—meaning that you did or said what you were prompted to do or say—then it "worked out" perfectly, regardless of how the person responded to what you did or said. Don't *ever* let the enemy convince you that, because you didn't see the results you had expected to see, it really wasn't a prompting from God.

I would tell my missionaries things like this: "Regarding the guy who treated you poorly at the door, you never know what will happen next. Maybe he will feel bad about having treated you that way and will stop the next missionaries he sees and listen to them. Or perhaps he will go to work the next day and tell a friend from work about what happened, and that friend will be a member of the Church and it will lead to a great conversation. In some cases, we will never know why God wanted us to follow that prompting. We just need to remember that we did what God wanted and leave the rest up to Him."

All we are expected to do is to act on the promptings that we get from the Holy Ghost. *The rest is not up to us.* We need to control the things that are in our control and not worry about the rest. What *is* under our control is to act immediately on the promptings from the Holy Ghost when they come. So let's do that!

Following Promptings Can Bring Challenging Results

Although the scriptures don't specify it, I believe that Nephi was following a prompting when he tried to counsel his elder brothers regarding their rudeness on the boat on the way to their new home. Yet it didn't work out that well for Nephi! His brothers bound him with strong cords for three days. But I'm sure counseling his brothers was still exactly what the Lord wanted Nephi to do.

After being chased out of Ammonihah, Alma was told to return and preach there again. As a result, the evil leaders in the city killed many innocent people and imprisoned Alma and Amulek. But Alma had done *exactly* what God had wanted him to do.

Abinadi followed the Lord's direction to return in disguise and teach the people of King Noah again. In this case, it led to his own death. I guess someone could say, "Well, *that sure didn't work out*!" But, in all reality, we know that it worked out *exactly* as God knew it would and that Abinadi did *exactly* what God wanted him to do.

And, in the greatest example of following God in spite of what will happen, we have the example of our elder brother, Jesus Christ. In His case, He knew what was ahead in Gethsemane and Golgotha. But that didn't stop Him. He followed through—*perfectly*—anyway!

We can cite many other instances where following the promptings didn't bring a "happily ever after" ending. We just need to trust that if we are following the promptings from the Holy Ghost, we are doing what the Lord wants and, as a result, we are *always* doing the right thing. I like to remember what my mom taught us about how she followed through on promptings: "When it doesn't work out like I expected it would, I just smile, shrug my shoulders, knowing that I did what God wanted . . . and then I move on."

Paul Harvey and "The Rest of the Story"

Only the older readers of this book will remember Paul Harvey, a famous radio personality from the 1950s through the early 2000s. When I was a teenager, I loved to listen to him on the radio twice a day. One summer, when I worked as a painter, I would take my lunch break every day—Monday through Friday—right at the time that

Paul Harvey's *News and Comment* was starting. I loved to listen to it while I ate my lunch. After work, as I drove home, I would listen to Paul Harvey's *The Rest of the Story*, where he would share amazing backstories about famous people or events.

This is how I feel about our responsibility to follow the promptings from the Holy Ghost: We are always supposed to act on them, even though, in many cases—actually, in most cases—we won't get to see how the story ends. In most situations, we will just need to do what my mom taught us and shrug our shoulders, smile, and move on, knowing that we did what God had wanted us to do. I like to tell people the following: "When it comes to following promptings, it isn't like Paul Harvey. We don't always get to know 'the rest of the story.'" (While this analogy works great with people of my age or older, it didn't work so well when I shared it with eighteen- and nineteen-year-old missionaries!)

We May Never Know—On This Side of the Veil

I cannot tell you how many times I taught the above principle to the missionaries in our mission—about not worrying if it doesn't look like it worked out when we act on a prompting from the Holy Ghost. Yet the *same* missionaries would have those *same* doubts again and again. I tried to convince them to just keep acting on them and not worry. However, it was difficult for them because they kept having what they deemed to be "bad results." I explained to them that, in some cases, the success of our actions or words will only be made manifest at a later time, or we may not ever learn the results in this life at all. In many cases, we won't get to know "the rest of the story" until we are on the other side of the veil—and we need to be okay with that.

As a matter of fact, if you think about it, that is *exactly* what happened to Abinadi. He did everything that God wanted him to do but ended up dying without seeing any success in his preaching to King Noah and his wicked priests. Alma tried to keep them from killing Abinadi but then had to flee out of their presence to save his own life. Abinadi died as a martyr for Christ without knowing "the rest of the story." But, oh, how he must have rejoiced on the other side of the veil when he saw that his preaching converted Alma. Then, after his conversion, that one convert of his—Alma—converted many of the king's people and later accomplished even more great work in building up the kingdom of God on the earth.

So, as it turns out, Abinadi was an *amazingly* successful missionary. He just never got to see the results of his great work until he was on the other side of the veil. This is exactly what happens to us as we continue to act on those first promptings that we receive from the Holy Ghost. This will be one of the great rewards that we have to look forward to on the other side of the veil if we determine to be tools in God's hands here on earth. It will be so fun to have all of those results revealed to us as we learn "the rest of the story"! It's exciting just to think about.

Yet, even after teaching this principle to my missionaries over and over, many of these great missionaries would still be confused and full of doubts as they felt inspired to clap at a house, stop someone on the street, or say something during a lesson and it didn't "end well." Because of this, many of them became convinced that it was just their own crazy thoughts that drove them to do what they had done or to say what they had said. However, one time, I *finally* was given a *proof statement* that I was able to share with them:

The Door That Was Never Answered

One night, as I was interviewing a woman for baptism, I asked the question that I always liked to ask as I began those interviews—how she got to know the Church and meet our missionaries. She responded, "I love these missionaries, but they are not the reason that I am being baptized."

I said, "Oh really? Then, please tell me. Why are you being baptized?"

She replied, "One day, I was at home, praying to God. Well, I can't really say that I was praying to Him. I was kind of yelling at Him. It seemed that either He really didn't exist . . . or, if He did exist, He had certainly forgotten about me and didn't care at all about my welfare. My life was at its lowest point. I decided that I wanted proof that He existed and that He cared for me. So I told God that if He existed, I needed Him to send His angels to visit me.

"I had not even finished praying, when I heard a clap outside my door. I got up from my knees and peeked outside in such a way that whoever it was wouldn't know I was there. It was two of your young missionaries. I was so scared that God would answer my prayers that quickly that I didn't dare answer the door. They clapped a few more times. In fact, I need to congratulate you. You taught these boys to be pretty persistent. I thought they would never leave. But they finally went on their way. The thought of them clapping at my door immediately after I prayed for God to send me His angels wouldn't leave my brain. In fact, right when they left, a thought popped into my head that said, 'Those were my angels.' But then I had another thought that popped into my head that told me that they couldn't have been His angels—that it was impossible for God to have inspired them to get to my door within seconds of when I said that in my prayer. It was humanly impossible to happen that fast!" [Author's note: Did you notice her explaining the two *Bings!* to me—even though she didn't know anything about them? She talked about the first *Bing!* of "Those were my angels!" and then the second *Bing!* that it wasn't humanly possible to happen that fast.] She continued, "I tried to convince myself that it had to be just an amazing coincidence. But for days—even weeks—afterwards, it consumed me. I kept having that thought come back into my mind, saying, 'Those were my angels!'

"Finally, one day, probably about three months later—just about three or four weeks ago now—I was walking down the street, and I saw two missionaries walking on the other side of the street coming up the hill that I was walking down, heading in my direction. It was these same two missionaries that have been teaching me now, preparing me for baptism. I had never seen them before, but I knew that they had to be two missionaries from your church because they all dress alike. I crossed the street and stopped them. They told me later that they knew something was different because people usually crossed the street to *avoid* them. Anyway, after I stopped them, before I could even say anything, I just started crying. They looked at me and waited for me to stop crying. When I could talk, I asked them, 'What do I need to do to join your Church?'"

What an amazing story! It was just what I needed to help drive this point home to our missionaries. In the next zone conferences, I was eager to share this story with the whole mission. After sharing the story, I said, "Now, I don't know which one of you felt inspired to clap at that home a few months back and then when nobody answered, you turned to your companion and said, 'Well, I guess it wasn't a prompting. I guess it was just my own crazy thought!' Whoever you are, let me say this: You walked away from that home thinking that you had been fooled and that it wasn't really a prompting, when, in fact, it *had been* a prompting. Now, listen to this next part very closely: You—the same missionary who thought it was just your crazy thought instead of a prompting—**are the reason that this woman was baptized**! And you never even met her! Don't you ever dare doubt a prompting from the Holy Ghost! Just act on it! And, if it doesn't turn out the way that you had expected, smile, shrug your shoulders, and move on, knowing that you did what God wanted you to do . . . and leave the rest up to Him!"

Then I said to the rest of the missionaries at each zone conference, "How many times have each of you stopped because you felt prompted to talk to someone or clap at a door and you were treated rudely or nobody answered the door and you felt like, 'Well, I guess that wasn't a real prompting from God; I guess it was just my own thought'? And, worse still, because of that experience, some of you started doubting when other promptings came to you—and didn't act on them. In reality, God *wanted* you to talk to the person or clap at that door. Just like in this case. Stop doubting God and His promptings. Don't ever doubt them!"

I then reiterated the great quote from President Dieter F. Uchtdorf, who served in the First Presidency at the time: "Doubt your doubts before you doubt your faith."[2] I told our missionaries that—similarly—they needed to *doubt their doubts before they doubt their promptings*!

Bishop Monson Invites a Father to Return to Church

President Thomas S. Monson shared a wonderful story about acting on promptings even if you don't see the end results for a while:

---

2. Uchtdorf, "Come, Join with Us," 23.

As a bishop **I felt prompted one day** to call on a man whose wife was somewhat active, as were the children. This man, however, had never responded. It was a hot summer's day when I knocked on the screen door of Harold G. Gallacher. I could see Brother Gallacher sitting in his chair reading the newspaper. "Who is it?" he queried, without looking up.

"Your bishop," I replied. "'I've come to get acquainted and to urge your attendance with your family at our meetings."

"No, I'm too busy," came the disdainful response. He never looked up. I thanked him for listening and departed the doorstep.

The Gallacher family moved to California shortly thereafter. Many years went by. Then, as a member of the Quorum of the Twelve, I was working in my office one day when my secretary called, saying, "A Brother Gallacher who once lived in your ward is here in the office and would like to talk to you."

I responded, "Ask him if his name is Harold G. Gallacher who, with his family, once lived at Vissing Place on West Temple and Fifth South."

She said, "He is the man."

I asked her to send him in. We had a pleasant conversation together concerning his family. He told me, "I've come to apologize for not getting out of my chair and letting you in the door that summer day long years ago." I asked him if he was active in the Church. With a smile, he replied: "I'm a counselor in my ward bishopric. **Your invitation to come out to church, and my negative response, so haunted me that I determined to do something about it.**"

Harold and I visited together on numerous occasions before he passed away. The Gallachers and their children filled many callings in the Church.[3]

I am sure that young Bishop Monson left that doorstep a bit chagrined. But, since he knew that he had been acting on a prompting,

3. Monson, "Sacred Call of Service," 55; emphasis added.

he probably consoled himself in knowing that he did exactly what God had wanted him to do. He left the rest up to God. And, as you read in the story, not only did the Holy Ghost prompt Bishop Monson to go pay that visit to Harold, but *after* Bishop Monson's visit, the Holy Ghost worked on Harold as well. It was indeed Bishop Monson's visit—even though he got a disdainful response from a man who wouldn't even get out of his chair—that led to this man returning to activity in the Church. What a wonderful story of the importance of *never* doubting a prompting—not even after a bad response comes from it. Just like Bishop Monson, we will all experience bad responses from people as we act on promptings. But we should learn from this story that we don't always know what will happen next. After we do our part, we need to trust that God will do His.

A Phone Call from the Sister Missionaries

It was a Tuesday night in São Paulo, Brazil. I had just finished a productive meeting with President Felix (the stake president of the Casa Grande Stake in São Paulo), his high councilor over missionary work, and our two zone leaders over that zone and stake. I had a great deal of love and respect for President Felix—as I did for all of the seven wonderful stake presidents with whom I was blessed to serve. They were all such faithful men and sacrificed so much of their lives for the gospel, for their Savior, and for the members in their respective stakes. As I was driving back to the mission home, I got a phone call from two of our wonderful sister missionaries. As I picked up the phone, I could tell that they were very emotional. They seemed almost scared and in a panic. I quickly asked them if they were safe. They confirmed that they were. I asked them if they had been mugged. They said that they had not been. At this point, I calmed down a bit.

They said, "President, thank you for teaching us to follow the promptings of the Spirit."

I said, "That is great to hear. But now I'm anxious to hear what happened that caused you to want to call and thank me. Something happened, right?"

They said they had just finished a wonderful lesson with a family that they had been preparing for baptism. The Spirit had been very strong during the lesson, and they left the home, almost floating on a cloud. They needed to hurry home in order to be back in their home by the appropriate time that is required of all missionaries. As they were walking home, they began to walk down the same street that they always used to go home when, immediately, *they both had the same distinct impression hit them very hard that they should not go down that street.* One of the sister missionaries stopped, and the other stopped immediately afterward and said, "Something's wrong."

The companion said, "Yes. We are not supposed to go down this street."

The other sister said, "I felt the same thing. But if we don't go this way, we will be late getting home. This is the fastest way home." Even as she said that, they both knew that it didn't matter. They knew that they should not go down that street. It had always been a safe street with plenty of lighting and, usually, plenty of people. But that night, *the Spirit made it abundantly clear to both of them* that they were not to go down that street. They walked the longer way home and walked as fast as they could.

They made it home a little bit after the hour and were calling me to report in. (We had a rule in the mission that if a set of missionaries got in later than the correct hour, they needed to report in to let me know that they were safely home.)

These two great sister missionaries never did find out what would have happened to them had they gone down that street that night like they had always done. But they knew *without a doubt* that it was not safe for them to go down that street that night! I'm very grateful that they listened and acted on that prompting and didn't worry about not knowing what would have happened.

There Is Always Time for Promptings of the Holy Ghost

Sister Acuña was one of the most humble and diligent missionaries that I ever met. She was very close to the Spirit—you could tell by the way she engaged in her missionary work and the wonderful spirit you felt when you were with her. This is a story that happened near the end of her mission that she shared with me recently:

I was reaching the end of my mission—I think I had three months left—when I went on divisions with one of the sister training leaders in the mission. I was kind of excited about that because I felt that I could "rest" for the day and allow her (Sister Anhanha) to do all of the planning, since we were in her area. She had some important appointments that she had made previously, so we had plenty of work to do that day. She and her companion, Sister Andreasen, were two very powerful missionaries that I really admired.

We were rushing to get from place to place, and also trying to reach every goal we had set for the day. It was a good day, we were focused, and we were excited to be working together. As we were walking down the street of a very steep hill, we saw a group of teenage girls who were laughing and chatting. After we walked past them, I felt very strongly that we should go back to talk to them. For a moment I doubted because I had a lot of other thoughts that came into my head immediately after that thought. Those other thoughts were, "This isn't even my area," and "We are in too big of a hurry. We don't have time to stop right now. It will just make us later and we can't afford that." But I knew we needed to stop and talk to them.

I said, "Sister Anhanha, I want to talk to those girls." We went back, introduced ourselves, and invited them to church. We got their addresses and, for me, that was the end of it. I was happy that I followed that strong impression that I was given—that urgency that I felt to talk to them. Even though nothing "spectacular" happened, I didn't let the doubts come into my mind about having stopped. I knew it had been the right thing to do and I felt good about it. I thought that was the last I would ever hear or know about that experience. The next day, I was back in my area with my companion and I forgot all about it.

A month or so later, in one of our zone meetings, I was blessed to hear "the rest of the story." In our zone meeting that day, we were sharing miracles with each other from the previous week (as we always did). Sister Anhanha got up and started telling her miracle. I wasn't expecting to hear something that had to do with me. She told about the day that I had stopped to talk to some girls in the street, and that she and her companion went to their houses and started teaching them, but one of the addresses was wrong so they searched for this one girl until they found her house.

It turned out that this girl and her family, along with a couple of her friends, accepted the invitation to be baptized. In total, seven people were going to be baptized that week, and other family members were being taught as well, getting ready to be baptized! Sister Anhanha started crying as she told the story to us missionaries in that meeting, saying that if it were not for me, they would never have found those elect families.

Of course, it's not me who is important in this story, but I had never felt so strongly that I was indeed an instrument in the hands of God, and that testimony forever changed me. I am so grateful that my mission president taught us to recognize and follow our first prompting and to ignore the second prompting that tries to talk us out of acting on the first prompting. This story also reminds me of that wonderful quote we heard on our mission that "we can count how many seeds are in an apple, but we cannot count how many apples are in a seed." It is so neat to think of how many lives and generations will be impacted by one small decision to act on a prompting to go back and talk to a group of teenage girls. I'm so grateful that I got to hear how this story ended.

They Probably Never Knew How Much They Helped

In a wonderful devotional at BYU–Hawaii, Jared Anderson told the following story from the lives of his direct ancestors:

> I would like to share a story of James and Drusilla Hendricks. They are my great, great, great grandparents. They were a young married couple when they joined the church in 1835. They gathered with the saints in Missouri and settled in Clay County. In Missouri at that time, there was a lot of persecution and conflict between members of the Church

who were gathering there and the other settlers. In one such conflict, which has been called the Battle of Crooked River, James Hendricks was shot in the back by the mob and was paralyzed from the neck down. . . .

The young Hendricks family sold what they could and left their home and their farm in Missouri. They crossed the Mississippi river into Quincy, Illinois, where they found shelter in a temporary dugout home. Within a few weeks of arriving in Quincy, they ran out of food and faced starvation. In her own words Drusilla said, "I had one spoonful of sugar and one saucer full of corn meal. I made mush of the meal and put the sugar on it and gave it to my children. That was the last of the eatables of any kind we had in the house or on the earth. We were in a strange land among strangers. I went to work and washed everything and cleaned the house thoroughly as I said to myself, 'If I die, I will die clean.'"

Not long after, they were visited by a neighbor, Reuben Allred. ***He had a feeling that the Hendricks family was out of food and was prompted by the spirit to bring them a sack of flour***. Because of this, the family was able to survive. They lived sparingly for another two weeks, but eventually found themselves again in the same condition. They had nothing and were on the verge of starvation, yet again.

As she had done before, Drusilla decided to wash and clean their home, and then wait to die. She was just finishing cleaning the doorstep when another neighbor, Alexander Williams, came with two bushels of meal on his shoulders. He said he was busy working on his own crops ***when the spirit spoke to him saying, "Brother Hendricks' family is suffering." He immediately dropped everything he was doing and came running.***

Brother Allred and Brother Williams were instruments in the hands of God. They lived worthy of the Spirit, they were receptive to the promptings, and **most importantly, they acted on the spiritual promptings they received**. The Hendricks family was provided for and preserved in their most critical and trying time.

> Elder Rasband said, "The Lord knows the needs of all His children—and He knows who is prepared to help. If we let the Lord know in our morning prayers that we are ready, He will call on us to respond. If we respond, He will call on us time and time again."[4]

What a great story! It is impressive to me that these men, probably both without a lot to spare for themselves during those trying times, got the promptings and acted on them *immediately*. Although they both knew that they needed to help, I doubt that either one of them knew that this family was literally about to starve to death.

We may never know—at least not on this side of the veil—the end results of the good that we will do by following the promptings of the Spirit. But, once we have our own testimony of the importance of immediately following the promptings of the Spirit, we really don't need to worry about that anymore—and it can give us just one more reason to be excited for what lies ahead for us on the other side of the veil as we will then get to learn "the rest of the story."

---

4. Anderson, "Acting on Spiritual Promptings"; emphasis added.

CHAPTER 9

What If the Prompting Doesn't Make Sense?

"When you get an impression, act upon it, however unusual it seems or however inadequate you feel in following it. Act upon it. There's a reason. You may not know the reason, but blessings will follow to you and to someone else if you hear Him."

—President Dallin H. Oaks[1]

I love the story found in 2 Kings 6:15–17, where Elisha and his servant are surrounded by host of horses and chariots. Things looked very bleak for them. But then Elisha shows his servant the heavenly host that was there to protect and help them.

> And when the servant of the man of God was risen early, and gone forth, behold, an host compassed the city both with horses and chariots. And his servant said unto him, **Alas, my master! how shall we do?** And he answered, **Fear not: for they that be with us are more than they that be with them**. And Elisha prayed, and said, Lord, I pray thee, open his eyes, that he may see. And the Lord opened the eyes of the young man; and he saw: and, **behold, the mountain**

---

1. Oaks, "How I Hear Him."

was full of horses and chariots of fire round about Elisha" (emphasis added).

Elisha's faith allowed him to see what the servant could not see. If Elisha had not been able to see what was there, it wouldn't change the fact that the Lord had placed those "horses and chariots of fire" to fill the mountain. But without seeing that vision, it would have seemed impossible that the prophet and his servant would come away victorious. **You see, because we can only see with our physical eyes, it may often seem that what the Spirit is prompting us to do is crazy.**

In Isaiah 55:8–9, we read: "For my thoughts are not your thoughts, neither are your ways my ways, saith the Lord. For as the heavens are higher than the earth, so are my ways higher than your ways, and my thoughts than your thoughts." We all know that God knows all things. Yet, we still continue to doubt and hold back on acting on promptings when they don't seem to make sense to us. We need to get past this challenge.

According to John Taylor, Joseph Smith was well acquainted with this principle and even taught it to him. He, in fact, wrote that the Prophet Joseph told him the following: "Elder Taylor, you have been baptized, you have had hands laid upon your head for the reception of the Holy Ghost, and you have been ordained to the holy Priesthood. ***Now, if you will continue to follow the leadings of that spirit, it will always lead you right. Sometimes it might be contrary to your judgment; never mind that, follow its dictates;*** and if you be true to its whisperings it will in time become in you a principle of revelation, so that you will know all things."[2] We would be able to do so much more good in the world if we would learn to follow this wise counsel from Joseph Smith.

God Doesn't Need to Use Logic

This is one important principle that I drove home over and over with our missionaries. After helping them understand how the Spirit

2. Young, *Journal of Discourses*, 19:154; emphasis added.

works—and warning them about the second voice—I emphasized three additional important principles:

1. Act immediately on every prompting.
2. Don't doubt your promptings. Just act on them and move on.
3. Don't worry if the prompting doesn't make sense.

This third principle was a tough one to get many of the missionaries to buy into. Since the adversary does such a great job of coming in as the second voice and convincing people of just how little sense that original prompting makes, it is very important that we don't worry about the "logic"*—or lack thereof*—of any prompting from the Holy Ghost. We just need to act on it. You see, the benefit that God has is that He already knows how things will end up. He knows what the right thing to do is, and sometimes that "right thing" won't appear to make any sense at all to us. Do you think that matters to Him? Of course not. However, Satan will try to use logic to show us why it makes no sense to act on that first prompting.

God Loves the Crazies

During our time in Brazil, every year—as with all missions in the world—we were blessed to have a member of one of the quorums of the Seventy visit our mission, performing what has been referred to as a "mission tour." One year, our mission tour was presided over by Elder Claudio Campos. One of the outstanding messages that he shared with our mission was that "God loves the crazies!" His wonderful message was that God will often ask His servants to do something that doesn't make any sense. In fact, it may seem like it is impossible to us. But we just need to trust in Him and move forward, allowing Him to do the hard part, once we show our faith in Him and do our part. **"Impossible" is oftentimes His starting point**! Elder Campos told our missionaries that God needs more people who are willing to act on promptings that don't make sense so that God can touch—and save—many more lives. God loves those who move forward with faith in this regard. Elder Campos then shared with our missionaries many great examples from the scriptures:

1. Moses and the crossing of the Red Sea in Exodus 14:21–22.
2. Moses and the brass serpent in Numbers 21.
3. Joshua and the conquering of the city of Jericho in Joshua 6:20.
4. Noah and the building of the ark on dry ground in Genesis 6–8.
5. Gideon reducing his army to only 300 men in Judges 7.
6. Elijah and the 450 prophets of Baal in 1 Kings 18.
7. A young man or woman leaving family and friends to serve a mission for their church.

He gave many more examples, and he had the perfect attention of every missionary in the chapel that day. I distinctly remember how strong the Spirit was in that meeting as he challenged our missionaries to be bolder in their work—to be fearless in following God's promptings—and to realize that God can do anything He wants. We simply need to seek His promptings every day and to act on them as soon as they come, without stopping to wonder if the prompting makes sense. What a great message for all of us to hear and internalize.

The Spirit Will Use a "Bank Shot" When Necessary

I played college basketball for a small college about eight years after the legendary UCLA basketball coach John Wooden retired. Coach Wooden was very particular about every detail, and he drilled his players daily on performing those details perfectly. One of the things that he had his players do that pretty much nobody else did—and it still is rarely done to this day—was to use the bank shot. A bank shot is where, instead of a player shooting the ball directly into the basket, he shoots it so that it bounces off the backboard and into the basket. Wooden was convinced that in many areas of the court, it was actually a higher percentage shot than just trying to make the shot straight on. In fact, in some of his drills, if a player made the basket but it wasn't a bank shot, the basket didn't count.

One of the interesting things about the bank shot is that—especially when people aren't used to seeing it done—it may appear to anyone watching the game that the shot is going to miss by a lot, but then it goes in.

Oftentimes, the Lord's promptings will do the same thing. He may prompt us to do one thing, only to have us later discover that the real reason we were prompted to do what we did was for a completely different reason, or for a different person, than we had originally thought. I love the following story from our mission. From it we learn just how important it is to act on every prompting, no matter how "highly illogical" it seems to be. It is also a great example of how the Lord at times will use a figurative "bank shot" to accomplish His purposes.

Sister Courtney Gunnerson (now Courtney Corbin) was an amazingly diligent, hardworking, faith-fillled missionary. One day, she and her companion were very busy with many people to visit. All of a sudden, Sister Gunnerson had a thought pop into her head (*Bing!*) that said, "We need to go visit Kelvin." Kelvin was a recent convert they had been working with. Immediately after the first thought came into her head, another thought came (*Bing!*) that said, "No. Kelvin is at school right now. Plus we already have a very busy day scheduled. We don't have time to do this." But then Sister Gunnerson remembered what I had taught about never doubting the promptings of the Holy Ghost. We should act on them, even when they don't make sense, and we should avoid listening to the logic of the second voice.

So Sister Gunnerson told her companion, "We need to go see Kelvin right now." Her companion voiced all of the same concerns that Sister Gunnerson had already thought of (about him being at school and them not having time). But Sister Gunnerson was committed to act on this prompting even though it didn't make sense. So off they went to Kelvin's house. When they got there, Kelvin's mom answered the door. The sister missionaries asked for Kelvin. Kelvin's mom replied that he was at school. I'm not sure what Sister Gunnerson's companion told her when that happened, but I know that a lot of companions would have said, "Told you so."

However, Sister Gunnerson *was certain* that they were there for a reason. She just didn't know what that reason was. She wasn't about to give up. She turned around and saw a little boy—maybe four or five years old—sitting on the curb. She went over to the boy and asked, "Do you know a nice family that we could invite to our church?" The boy, without even opening his mouth, pointed to a house on the street that was just a few doors away from Kelvin's house. Sister Gunnerson felt something that told her that she should go to that house. She and her companion went over to that home and clapped. A woman answered. About three weeks later, the woman who answered the door (Dina) and her husband and two children were baptized.

Later, Dina shared with Sister Gunnerson that before the missionaries showed up at her door, she had been praying for someone purer than her to come and guide her to a new level of happiness. She told Sister Gunnerson that she was the answer to those prayers. She also told the sister missionaries that the day that they clapped at her home, she never even heard anyone clapping—she actually heard someone calling out her name! That was the reason she answered the door, because she normally would never answer the door for strangers. The sisters knew that no one had called her name. They didn't even know her name. The Lord was doing His work!

Sister Gunnerson was so grateful that she had learned to act on that first prompting—even though it may not make any sense. You see, God *knew* that Dina needed the missionaries at her home right at that time. However, He also knew that the sister missionaries didn't know Dina or where she lived. So He prompted them to go to Kelvin's house—a prompting that didn't make any sense—and He took care of the rest. I love that the Holy Ghost wasn't worried about the fact that Sister Gunnerson had no idea how to get to Dina's home. He knew that Dina needed the missionaries, so he used what he had at his disposal. He knew that she knew where Kelvin lived and, since that was just a few houses away from Dina, that was close enough for him. It is so neat to see how God and the Spirit work. We can be part of miracles as we act on promptings.

Every one of us can think of times where we have had a *Bing!* come to our mind, but because the prompting didn't make sense—even though it was a good prompting—we didn't act on it. We need to train ourselves differently. We need to remember that Heavenly Father doesn't need to have things make sense. He already *knows* what the right thing to do is, so when we get a prompting to do something good—*even when it seems not to make any logical sense*—we need to believe that just as the Prophet Joseph taught, nine times out of ten, it will be right. We just need to act on it and trust that it is from God.

Overcome Your Own Desires and Act on Those Promptings

Elder William Mercês Silva was an outstanding and very faithful elder in our mission and the oldest of nine children in his family. This story happened before he served with us, but he shared it with me after the mission:

> In my last year at home before leaving for the mission field, in order to prepare for a full-time mission, I made a series of commitments that made my life very hectic. I worked in the morning to pay for the mission expenses. This was followed by a technical course in high school. Right after school, I had seminary. As soon as seminary was over, I went to a language course (alternating one day with English class and the other, Italian). I would run from that class to get to a driving school in order to be authorized to drive, if necessary, on my mission. I would then get home around midnight only to go study for school and seminary classes for the next day. Then, I would try to get some sleep so that I could start that routine all over again the next morning at 6 a.m. I was always exhausted. I urgently needed some rest.
>
> Finally, one day I was released early from school and was going home, anxious to get some sleep, when I had a prompting—not something I heard, but something that I *felt*. It said, "Go to Lucas' house." But that second voice came almost immediately after. I'm not sure if it was the adversary or me, but I remember feeling, "But I really need to rest! I deserve to rest!"
>
> In response, that heavenly command was repeated in my mind, "Go to Lucas's house." This time, another, different negative response immediately followed: "But I don't know where Lucas's house is, since he recently moved!"
>
> This time, the feeling I got was, "I'm God. Do you not know that I can show you where his house is? You are the president of the Young Men organization in your ward. How

do you expect the boys to learn to follow the Spirit if you won't follow it?'

With that last *Bing!* I turned my motorcycle around and accelerated in the opposite direction of my house, not really knowing where I was going. As I rode, I saw another young man from our ward, sitting in the square. I stopped and asked him what he was doing.

He replied, "I don't know. I was at home and I felt the Spirit tell me that I needed to go to the square. I remember thinking that I had no reason to come here, but then the thought came again. So I came, but I didn't know what to do when I got here, so I just sat down."

"Do you know where Lucas's new home is?" I asked him. He replied that he did. I then told him that I knew why God sent him to the square. I told him to get on the back of my motorbike. He did, and off we went to Lucas's house.

As soon as we pulled up to Lucas's house, the door opened and Lucas was leaving his home with a very angry expression. However, as soon as he saw us, his face changed to joy and he asked us to come in. He told us that he was in trouble and had been praying for help. He felt that his prayer was not being answered and decided to stop praying and leave the house, furious at God and at the Church. However, when he found us pulling up to his house as he was leaving, he knew that we were the answer to his prayers and that God had not abandoned him.

How grateful I am that, in spite of how tired I was and without really knowing any reason as to why I should do it, I chose to follow that prompting. I'm also grateful that another young man (João Pedro) followed his prompting so he could help me be the answer to Lucas's prayers. I don't know what would have happened if we both didn't follow the Spirit, but I know that the Lord blessed me to have the strength to follow promptings. This habit (of following promptings) was something that also helped me many different times as I served my mission.

The Book of Mormon in the Wrong Language

Elder Thomas Richins was a missionary with a huge heart. I got to know him extremely well on the mission, and one thing that always impressed me about him was how much he cared about the happiness and well-being of others. One day, Elder Richins was at the distribution center of the São Paulo Temple. Even though Portuguese is the only language in Brazil, Elder Richins all of a sudden had a strange—and strong—urge to buy a copy of the Book of Mormon in French. This made absolutely no sense at all. He didn't speak French. He would have no use for such a book. He even asked himself why in the world he would want the Book of Mormon in French. He remembers thinking, "Well, French is somewhat similar to Portuguese. Perhaps if I get this Book of Mormon in French, it may give me a chance to learn a new language." So, without any further thought, he bought it.

Just one short week later, Elder Richins and his companion met a woman from Haiti. They taught her and gave her a copy of the Book of Mormon. Later, on a return appointment, when they asked her about her reading of the Book of Mormon, she expressed a great deal of frustration with the Portuguese language. It was obvious to them that she was beginning to "tune out" their message because of her frustration. It was then that Elder Richins remembered that he had a copy of the Book of Mormon in her native tongue of French.

The next day, the elders returned to her home with this surprise "gift." Her demeanor completely changed. She was excited to read it. With tears in her eyes, she told the elders how much she loved and treasured that special book. She was soon baptized and loved attending church every Sunday. All because of the *Bing!* that an elder received to buy a copy of the Book of Mormon in the wrong language!

An Illogical Prompting That Saved 100 Lives

Wilford Woodruff once told a story about a strong prompting that saved his life and the lives of about one hundred other Saints. He wrote:

> When I got back to Winter Quarters from the pioneer journey [1847], President [Brigham] Young said to me, "Brother Woodruff, I want you to take your wife and children and go to Boston and stay there until you can gather every Saint of God in New England and Canada and send them up to Zion."
>
> I did as he told me. It took me two years to gather up everybody, and I brought up the rear with a company (there were about one hundred of them). We arrived in Pittsburgh one day at sundown. We did not want to stay there, so I went to the first steamboat that was going to leave. I saw the captain and engaged passage for us on that steamer. I had only just done so when the spirit said to me, and that, too, very strongly, "Don't go aboard that steamer, nor your company." Of course, I went and spoke to the captain, and told him I had made up my mind to wait.
>
> Well, that ship started, and had only got five miles [eight kilometers] down the river when it took fire, and three hundred persons were burned to death or drowned. If I had not obeyed that spirit and had gone on that steamer with the rest of the company, you can see what the result would have been.

Sometimes the Promptings Make No Sense and Feel Awkward to Follow

My youngest sister, Mindy Carter, has had many experiences with acting on promptings that don't make sense—and even experiences with acting on promptings that can seem a little bit awkward. Fortunately for those whose lives she has blessed, Mindy has never been afraid of "awkward"!

When Mindy's daughter Cassie was on a mission, the bishop of the ward where Cassie was serving felt impressed (*Bing!*) to contact a single woman in the ward who had been less active for several years and ask her if she would consider having the sister missionaries live with her. The woman quickly gave him a resounding "NO." The bishop asked her to go home and pray about it, which she did. To her own surprise, she felt like it was the right thing to do. She ended up calling the bishop to accept, even though she still had reservations about doing so.

When Cassie arrived at the woman's house, they had a wonderful first visit. The good sister took an instant liking to Cassie (Sister Carter) and her companion.

Over the weeks that she lived there, Sister Carter would often leave Post-it notes around the house for her landlady to find (in the microwave, on the fridge, and so on), telling this sweet woman how much she loved and appreciated her. They had many conversations that ranged from meaningful to silly, and they even had private jokes together. They became dear friends.

One day, a few weeks after Cassie had been transferred to another area, this woman popped into Mindy's mind (*Bing!*) with the thought that she should call her. Mindy thought, "That's silly! I've never even spoken to this woman before. And now, my daughter doesn't even live with her. It makes no sense to call her. Also, I don't have her phone number, and I don't even know her last name to try and look it up—I couldn't call her even if I wanted to." But then, after giving herself all of the reasons *not* to call, the thought came to her once again (*Bing!*). This time, though, along with the thought to call her, Mindy got a "reminder" that this woman had once texted a picture of Sister Carter to Mindy, back when Cassie had been with her.

With that extra thought, Mindy finally talked herself into placing this fairly strange, out-of-the-blue, and awkward phone call. She remembers thinking, "I don't even have any idea of what to say when she answers the phone, but here goes." (Bless Mindy's heart—that is always how she has been. She doesn't worry that she doesn't know what to say. She will just plow forward, full steam ahead into the "awkward.")

The woman answered the phone and Mindy said, "Hi. You don't know me, but I'm Sister Carter's mom." Mindy started to tell her that she just wanted to call and thank her again for being so good to her daughter during the time that she lived with her. However, before Mindy could get all of that out, the woman broke into tears. Eventually, after she regained her composure enough to talk, she told Mindy that she had been so sad ever since Cassie had been transferred. She went so far as to say, "I miss her so much. You just don't know." (Mindy resisted the urge to tell her that she was pretty sure she had a very good idea of how she felt about missing her daughter!)

This good woman then explained that she didn't feel the same connection with the new sisters that she had enjoyed when Cassie and her companion lived there. She missed that connection, which left her feeling lonely and uncomfortable in her own home. She told Mindy that, as she was speaking with her on the phone right then, she was sitting in her car in a parking lot because she didn't even have the emotional strength to go home and see these other sister missionaries who lived with her.

She went on to say that *right before Mindy had called her*, she was *pleading with her Heavenly Father*, telling Him how sad and lonely she felt and *asking Him if He even knew her or cared about her*. The last thing she said to her Heavenly Father before her phone rang was, "*Please just let me know that you care!*"

Because Mindy had the courage to act on a very awkward prompting, she was able to be the immediate answer to prayer for this sweet woman. We need to remember that this is how our Heavenly Father works. Since He knows what needs to be done, He has no need to worry about whether something makes sense or seems awkward.

Going to Get a Light Bulb at Dinnertime

In the October 2021 general conference, Elder Gary E. Stevenson shared a story about a man named Jens from Denmark. Here is his story in Jens's own words:

> We live in an idyllic, small, half-timbered house with a thatched roof, in the center of a cozy little village, close to the village pond. On this night with the most beautiful Danish summer weather imaginable, doors and windows were open, and everything breathed peace and quiet. Due to our gloriously bright and long summer nights, I had not been in a hurry to replace a burned-out light bulb in our utility room.
>
> Suddenly, I got a strong feeling that I had to replace it immediately! At the same time, I heard my wife, Mariann,

> call for me and the children to wash our hands because dinner was ready!
>
> I had been married long enough to know that this was not the time to start doing anything else than washing my hands, but I heard myself calling out to Mariann that I would just pop over to the store to buy a new light bulb. I felt a strong urge to leave immediately.
>
> The grocery store was only on the other side of the pond. We usually walked, but today I grabbed my bike. While riding past the pond, out of the corner of my eye I noticed a small boy, about two years old, walking alone near the edge of the pond, very close to the water—suddenly he fell in! One minute he was there—and the next he was gone!
>
> No one had seen this happen but me. I threw my bike on the ground, ran, and jumped into the waist-high pond. The surface of the water immediately closed with duckweed, making it impossible to see through the water. Then I sensed a movement to one side. I put my arm in the water, got hold of a T-shirt, and pulled the little boy up. He started gasping, coughing, and crying. Soon afterward the boy was reunited with his parents.[3]

It didn't make sense to go buy a light bulb when his wife was calling the whole family together for dinner. But, oh what a difference it made!

Fresh Crab and French Bread

I saved this story for the final one in this chapter because it is one of my favorite stories about following the promptings of the Spirit *even when they don't make any sense.* My mom loved this story and was the one who first brought it to my attention. It was shared by a member of the Church by the name of Garnee Faulkner in the June 1985 *Ensign* in an article titled "Fresh Crab and French Bread." I hope this story touches you as it does me:

---

3. Stevenson, "Beautifully Simple," 47–48.

Garnee tells of a trip that she and her husband, Ron, made to San Francisco. When she saw the steaming vats of crab on Fisherman's Wharf, she had the sudden thought to take some to Emma, a grieving widow in their ward. She told Ron of her idea, but he was not in favor of such an odd gift, saying it would be too hard to transport, and suggested a simpler souvenir. They popped in and out of gift shops but never found the right memento.

Unsuccessful and weary, they headed for their car. However, on their way to the car, Garnee saw the crab vats again and repeated her desire to buy some for Emma. With assurance from the vendor that they could indeed transport the crab for the 150-mile journey home, Garnee purchased some crab that was securely wrapped in paper, as well as a loaf of the wharf's famous French bread.

On the drive home, Garnee's mind turned to Emma. It was only ten months earlier that Emma, her husband, Ed, and their oldest son, David, all spoke in sacrament meeting. Days later, after taking David to the Missionary Training Center, Ed suffered a fatal heart attack while still in Utah. He left behind Emma and their six children (their youngest was just a toddler). His loss was felt deeply in the community as well, since Ed had been a respected surgeon.

Many grieved for the family, but most people didn't know how to reach out and help, since Emma was quite reserved. Few knew her well. Time went by, but her sorrow remained. Between her grief and some health issues, Emma became more and more homebound. But Garnee was determined to be her friend, refusing to be dissuaded by the unpredictable manner in which Emma received her from one visit to the next. She continued to try to visit Emma every week. Occasionally, she would be invited in. Oftentimes, she was simply met at the door, with Emma quickly ending the visit by saying, "Thank you for coming."

That day, as Garnee rang the bell, she heard the pitter patter of many little feet. Emma opened the door, surrounded by her children, and gave her a confused look as she said, "Yes?"

Garnee felt a bit disheartened with her cool one-word reception, but she plowed forward with forced enthusiasm, gushing about their trip to the city and her desire to bring something back for her. As she took the fresh crab and French bread, Emma asked, "Is this for any special occasion?"

Garnee replied, "No, I just thought you might enjoy some crab from the wharf."

Emma thanked her with a puzzled expression and closed the door. Garnee returned to the car, discouraged. She slumped down in her seat, and she and Ron drove home in silence. She wondered if she had made a mistake in giving her such a strange gift. Maybe Emma didn't even like crab! She felt terrible for the next couple of days.

However, two days later, Garnee received a letter from Emma in the mail. It began by saying how touched she was with the kind gesture, and that she wanted to share some thoughts with her about the gift. She described how that day had started in the usual way with the usual routines. Then, as she was outside sweeping the walkways, she looked up to the heavens and asked, "Ed, do you know what day this is? Do dates have a meaning in heaven? Can you possibly know how much you are missed; how I long to be taken into your strong arms and held again just for a minute?" She cried as she continued to look up to the sky and asked him if he remembered that day twenty-three years ago, or even two years ago. She then recounted in her letter some of the many occasions when she and Ed had gone to San Francisco. It had become their special place. Ed loved to learn as much as he could about the field of medicine and would arrange to attend seminars there so that he and Emma could end their stay by going to the wharf, where they would always buy a loaf of bread and a fresh crab. It became a symbol of their time spent together in San Francisco.

Emma went on to share how difficult that day had been two days ago (the day Garnee dropped off the loaf of bread and crab). In the afternoon, she received a beautiful floral arrangement with a card from her children, all declaring their love for her. She was so grateful for her wonderful children, and she was touched at their thoughtfulness. She realized that she was indeed blessed to have them, and how beautiful it was to see a part of Ed in each of them.

The letter ended with this: "Then at the close of the day, when I opened the door and saw you standing there with a loaf of bread and a package of fresh crab, it was like a direct message. You denied knowing it was a special day. Therefore, I felt it was Ed's way of saying, 'Happy anniversary. I do remember.'"[4]

What a touching story about the importance of acting on our promptings, even when they don't make sense. I pray that more and more of us will recommit ourselves each day, pleading with the Lord to trust us with at least one prompting for that day and promising Him that as He does send promptings to us, we will act *immediately* on that prompting, no matter how little sense it makes and no matter how awkward it makes us feel. Heavenly Father has so many children that He wants to bless and help. But He needs more of us to respond to our promptings. And it is so rewarding for those who do quickly act on their promptings.

Elder Holland put it very well when he said, "In spite of what we all feel are our limitations and inadequacies—and we all have challenges—nevertheless, may we labor side by side with the Lord of the vineyard, giving the God and Father of us all a helping hand with His staggering task of answering prayers, providing comfort, drying tears, and strengthening feeble knees. If we will do that, we will be more like the true disciples of Christ we are meant to be."[5] Not only will it change who we are—as we become "true disciples of Christ"—but it changes how we feel, as well. Just imagine how Garnee must have felt when she received that letter from Emma, thanking her for the fresh crab and French bread.

4. Faulkner, "Fresh Crab," 38–39.
5. Holland, "Strengthen Them," 103.

CHAPTER 10

Act on Your Promptings!

"Now ye may suppose that this is foolishness in me; but behold I say unto you, that by small and simple things are great things brought to pass; and small means in many instances doth confound the wise. And the Lord God doth work by means to bring about his great and eternal purposes; and by very small means the Lord doth confound the wise and bringeth about the salvation of many souls."

—Alma 37:6–7

We have already discussed many of Satan's strategies that he uses so successfully as he and his followers work against the promptings that we get from the Holy Ghost. Another strategy that he uses is that he will oftentimes get us to believe that the prompting we just got from the Holy Ghost is really *not all that important.* He wants us to feel that it is such a small thing that it really won't matter if we do it or not, so he will prompt us to ignore the prompting. We must *never* fall for that. This has been one of his most successful strategies that he uses regularly with millions of people. Think about the feelings that even many members of the Church have had on a daily basis when it comes to deciding whether to do the following things or not: reading their scriptures, saying their personal prayers, holding weekly family home evenings, attending the temple, or even going to church. His promptings will be something like, "It won't matter this one time," or "I'm in too much of a hurry to take the time to read or pray today." But overall, the thought or message from him is that "it's really not that big of a deal."

This is also how he gets people to begin to commit other sins, whether it be participating in pornography or breaking the Word of Wisdom, for example. It will be a thought like, "This one time won't hurt." Yet he is laughing as you listen to him because he knows that all he needs is for you to open the door a crack for this sin to start. In many cases, he will get you to become addicted to this sin in the near future, or—in the case of not doing those small "right" things—he will get you to develop the habit of *not* doing them.

Yes, rationalization and justification are great tools of his. And one of his favorite uses of these tools is to rationalize that it is so small of an act—for good or for bad—that it *really won't matter this one time*. For the bad, he gets us to do it because "one time won't hurt," and for the good, he gets us *not* to do it, because "it really won't matter if we do it or not."

Forward or Backward—But Never Standing Still

Elder David A. Bednar taught the following at a Ricks College (now BYU–I) devotional:

> We are prompted by the Holy Ghost every day to do ordinary and simple things. For example, we are prompted to say our personal prayers every morning and every night. We are prompted to study the scriptures. We are prompted to keep the commitments we made in connection with the Honor and Dress Codes. To the degree that we heed these simple promptings, then our capacity to recognize and respond to the Holy Ghost is increased. To the degree that we do not heed these simple promptings, then our capacity to recognize and respond to the Holy Ghost is decreased. **We are either progressing or regressing in our ability to recognize and respond to the Holy Ghost. There is no neutral ground; there is no standing still.**
>
> The law of the harvest is real; we cannot gather crops in the fall which we did not properly plant and cultivate during the spring and summer. And we cannot realistically expect to

> recognize "*big*" promptings if we consistently fail to heed the "*small*" ones. The Lord's pattern is to teach us " . . . *line upon line, precept upon precept, here a little and there a little* . . ." (2 Nephi 28:30). Thus, revelation from our Heavenly Father comes most frequently in small increments and, like all knowledge, is granted according to our preparation. Misguided attempts to get spiritually supercharged through unusually long prayers, lengthy and unwise fasting, and intensive, short-term temple attendance certainly are no substitute for gradual, consistent, and conscientious attention to the promptings of the Holy Ghost.[1]

Elder Bednar's point is that not only do those small promptings really matter—he even gave the examples of daily prayer and scripture study—but with our decisions to follow the promptings or not, we are either progressing or regressing in our ability to recognize and respond to the promptings of the Holy Ghost. He also taught that, by acting on small promptings, we will be preparing ourselves for bigger promptings that are yet to come. What great counsel to live by.

A Simple Text of a Photo

My younger sister, JoEllen Johnson, was looking for a photo that one of her daughters needed. She came across a number of photos of that daughter with her high school friends, including a few of a friend who had since passed away. The thought came to JoEllen's mind (*Bing!*), "If I were the mom of this girl, I would want every possible photo I could have of her." At that point, she had another thought (*Bing!*) that she would, at some later point, go get real photos made to send to this mother. Those real photos, after all, would be much better quality for her. Then, another *Bing!* came that told her she would probably never get around to getting those photos printed and that she should just take her phone out, take pictures of the photos, and text them to the mom of that deceased friend right then and there. She did, and immediately she received a text back from the mother, saying how much it meant to her to get the photos. As it turned out, that day

1. Bednar, "Receiving, Recognizing, and Responding"; emphasis added.

was the birthday of her deceased daughter, and she was just about to head over to the cemetery with flowers.

JoEllen was *so grateful* that she had acted on the simple thought that came to her mind to send them to that mom right away on what turned out to be a very special day. JoEllen didn't know it was that girl's birthday. But the Holy Ghost did!

Sometimes the Prompting Will Just Be to Pray

We need to act on every prompting that comes to us, even if it is just to get on our knees and pray for someone. The following three stories illustrate this point:

Graham W. Doxey and His Parents' Prayers

Elder Boyd K. Packer shared the following story:

> Elder Graham W. Doxey, who once served in the Second Quorum of the Seventy, told me of an experience. His mother, who was later a counselor in the Primary general presidency, also told me of this experience.
>
> During World War II, he was in the navy posted to China. He and several others went by train to the city of Tientsin to look around.
>
> Later they boarded a train to return to their base, but after more than an hour, the train turned north. They were on the wrong train! They spoke no Chinese. They pulled the emergency cord and stopped the train. They were put off somewhere in the countryside with nothing to do but walk back to the city.
>
> After walking for some time, they found a small pump-handle car, the kind that the railroad workers use. They set it in the rails and began to pump their way along the tracks. It would coast downhill, but it had to be pushed uphill.
>
> As they came to one steep downhill slope, they scrambled aboard the car and began to coast. Graham was the last to get aboard. The only place left for him was in the front of the car. He ran alongside and finally climbed aboard. As he did

so, he slipped and fell. He was bouncing on his back with his feet against the car to keep from being run over. As the car quickly gained speed, he heard his mother's voice say, 'Bud, you be careful!'

He wore heavy military boots. His foot slipped, and the thick sole of his boot caught in a gear of a wheel and stopped the car just one foot (30 cm) from his hand.

His parents, who were presiding over the East Central States Mission at the time, were sleeping in a hotel room. His mother sat up at about 2:00 in the morning and awakened her husband: 'Bud's in trouble!' They knelt by the bed and prayed for the safety of their boy.

The next letter he received said, 'Bud, what's wrong? What happened to you?'

He then wrote to tell them what had happened. *When they compared times,* ***at the very time he was bouncing along that track,*** *his parents were on their knees in the hotel room half a world away, praying for his safety.*

These experiences of prompting and prayer are not uncommon in the Church. They are part of the revelation our Heavenly Father has provided for us.[2]

My Sister JoEllen's Prayer for Me

A similar story to the one we just shared about Graham Doxey happened in my own life. One early morning (probably three or four o'clock), my younger sister, JoEllen, was fast asleep in her dorm room bed while Len and I—her older twin brothers—were serving our church missions in different parts of Brazil.

All of a sudden, JoEllen woke up with a start, with an overwhelming feeling that I was in trouble. She felt certain that my life was in danger. She immediately jumped onto her knees and began *pleading* with the Lord to protect and bless me. After long minutes of sobbing and pleading, she was given a certain feeling of peace that all would

2. Packer, "Prayer and Promptings," 45; emphasis added.

be well and that I was fine. With that, she went right back to bed and quickly fell back asleep.

Later that morning, after the day had started, JoEllen called Mom and asked if everything was okay with me. Mom said that she had not heard anything and asked why. JoEllen thought that was strange, and then she described what had happened.

Meanwhile, that very morning (Brazil was about five or six hours ahead of them, timewise), I was at the doctor's office. I had developed a severely ingrown toenail that had become infected. The doctor scheduled it as a simple outpatient procedure. However, for some reason, while he was performing the procedure, I passed out and, according to the doctor, I completely stopped breathing. Because it was an outpatient procedure—and we were in Brazil back in 1982—he did not have the equipment necessary to get me breathing again. He later told me that he didn't know if they would actually be able to get me to breathe again. He thought they had lost me. My companion was really worried, too. He said that the doctor was yelling, "BREATHE! BREATHE, [bleep] it!" as he pounded on my chest. After what seemed to be a very long time, my companion said that I finally started breathing again and everything ended up being okay.

Later, we figured out the exact day and time of this outpatient surgery. If our calculations were correct, it appears that JoEllen was awakened with the thought that my life was in danger at the time that I was in surgery—probably at the exact same time that I stopped breathing! Isn't it amazing how the Spirit works? I am so grateful for the Holy Ghost, a wonderful sister, and the power of her prayer!

Pray as If It All Depends on God . . . Then Do Your Part

While we do need to remember that God is in charge and we should act on the promptings to pray for His help, we should still do all we can to get the results that we know God wants. Elder Boyd K. Packer shared another story about prayer in the October 2009 general conference.

> That principle is illustrated by the story of a little girl. She was upset with her brother, who built a trap to catch sparrows.

Unable to get help, she said to herself, "Well, I'll pray about it." After her prayer, the little girl told her mother, "I know he is not going to catch any sparrows in his trap because I prayed about it. I'm *positive* he won't catch any sparrows!"

Her mother said, "How can you be so sure?"

She said, "After I prayed about it, I went out and kicked that old trap to pieces."[3]

The Birthday Lasagna

The author of this next story withheld her name, so we will call her Sister Smith. Her story is found in the August 2019 *Ensign* magazine. Her message is another great story of how *a little act can make a big difference*:

For quite a while, Sister Smith had felt the desire to share her love and the Lord's love by taking homemade bread or some other food to someone in her ward, but she had never done it. She loved to cook, but she rarely made large meals anymore, now that she and her husband were empty nesters. She typically made smaller meals to avoid having days and days of leftovers. One night she decided to make some lasagna. Instead of making one large pan, she made two smaller ones. Her thinking was that she and her husband could eat one and she could finally deliver some food by giving the other one to someone who could benefit from it. She called the Relief Society president, who suggested she take the lasagna to a woman in the ward. She was a single working mom with two small kids.

That afternoon, Sister Smith texted the mom and told her that she had made an extra lasagna and wanted to take it to her and her kids. The woman responded, texting, "That is so weird! Sure, that would be great!" Then, after a bit, the woman texted again, saying, "Did you know it was my birthday today?" Sister Smith replied that she didn't know. Then, the woman texted, "Well, happy birthday to me!"

When Sister Smith took the meal over, the mom had just returned home from work. Both she and her children seemed excited about the homemade meal. The next Sunday at church, this grateful sister found Sister Smith and, with tears in her eyes, told her that every year on her

---

3. Packer, "Prayer and Promptings," 46.

birthday, her grandmother had a tradition of making her lasagna. That sweet grandmother had just passed away the year before. This was going to be the first time she was not going to get that special lasagna dinner from her grandmother on her birthday. When Sister Smith, out of the blue, wanted to drop off lasagna for her birthday dinner, this sweet sister knew that the Lord truly was aware of her and loved her. Sister Smith ends her story with this powerful statement: "And it strengthened my testimony that if we make ourselves available to be an instrument in the Lord's hands, He will show us where we can serve."[4]

An MTC Study Group Leaving a "Comfort Zone"

Sister Katie Thornhill (now Hadlock) was as good of a missionary as I have ever met. Knowing her, I can certainly understand how the experience in this story would have been difficult for her. But, once again, it shows how a seemingly small thing can have a huge positive impact on someone's life:

> When I was a new missionary in the MTC, I had an experience with the Spirit that I will never forget. I was sitting in the classroom with my district during one of our "study blocks." These study blocks were periods of time we were given to study on our own, without our teacher present. Well, I had a pretty fun district of missionaries, and that day during our study block, one conversation led to another and before we knew it, the room had become quite loud, and we were definitely doing more talking than studying, myself included. Several minutes passed like this and we were having a great time with each other. But then, as fast and distinct as a bolt of lightning striking the earth, the Spirit prompted me to do something unexpected: I was prompted to urge everyone in the room to be quiet, stop talking, and get back to studying.
>
> I remember feeling surprised at that prompting because at the time our study block was quickly winding to a close, and I didn't see the difference ten minutes of study would

4. "The Birthday Lasagna," 66; emphasis added.

make for anyone. But God knew the world of difference those ten minutes would make for one missionary in that room. This particular missionary had been studying amidst the noise around him, and I had become so carried away in conversations that I hadn't noticed until then.

I knew that obeying this prompting would mean doing something out of my comfort zone. I am naturally a more reserved person and I have a quiet voice, and this would require me to raise my voice above all the others in order to get their attention. Although the thought of this made me feel uncomfortable, I could not deny that this was a prompting from the Spirit, and the thought of *not* obeying the prompting made me feel even more uncomfortable. So I chose to act on the prompting immediately.

Interestingly, it was amazing to me how, *as soon as I began acting on the prompting, any and all fear or insecurity I had going into it vanished completely.* I have since had many experiences like this throughout my life, and *it has taught me the literal power that comes to us when we choose to be instruments in the Lord's hands by following the promptings of the Spirit.*

Little did I know that the missionary who had been quietly studying was pages away from finishing the Book of Mormon for the first time in his life. He later told me that during those last minutes of study block—when all was quiet—he was able to pray and ask God if the Book of Mormon is true, and he received the answer right then and there that it is; he said it was in that moment that he first gained a testimony of the Book of Mormon. How grateful I am that I chose to follow the promptings of the Spirit of the Lord that day, and for what that experience taught me about my ability to truly be an instrument in the Lord's hands.

The Rest of the Story

Earlier in this book we talked about not being afraid to act and to not doubt when the results are not what we had expected or hoped for—because we may never really know how the story will end. In this next story, shared by Elder Gary E. Stevenson at the April 2017 general conference, he got to see how things would have ended up if his father had not acted. But whether he would have been able to see it or not, it wouldn't have changed the necessity for his dad to act on that seemingly small prompting that ended up making a big difference:

> When I was about 11 years old, my father and I went hiking on a hot summer day in the mountains near our home. As Dad hiked up the steep trail, I jumped from one large rock to another along the sides of the trail. Intending to climb one of the large rocks, I began to clamber to the top of it. As I did so, I was surprised when my dad grabbed me by my belt and quickly pulled me down, saying, "Don't climb on that rock. Let's just keep on the trail."
>
> Minutes later, as we looked down from higher up the trail, we were stunned as we saw a big rattlesnake basking in the sun on top of the very rock I had intended to climb.
>
> Later, as we were driving home, I knew Dad was waiting for me to ask, "How did you know the snake was there?" So I asked, and my question led to a discussion about the Holy Ghost and how the Holy Ghost can help us. I have never forgotten what I learned that day.
>
> Can you see how the Holy Ghost helped me? I am forever grateful that my father listened to the still, small voice of the Holy Ghost, as it may have saved my life.[5]

The Missionary and His Twenty-Mark Note

Elder Boyd K. Packer shared this story from his life that serves as a wonderful example of how a "little" prompting can make a *huge* difference in the lives of others.

In the early 1970s, Elder Packer received an assignment to go with then-Elder Thomas S. Monson to organize a servicemen's stake in Europe. They met at Berchtesgaden, Germany, high in the Bavarian Alps. It was an absolutely beautiful site that had originally been built

5. Stevenson, "How," 117.

as headquarters for Adolf Hitler. It seemed very fitting to organize a stake of Zion there, replacing the previous hatred with a gathering of faithful Saints.

After completing that stake organization and setting apart the new leaders, they were assigned to participate in a stake conference in Berlin, which meant that they first had to travel down from the Alps all the way to the airport in Munich. They arrived at the airport in plenty of time for their 10:00 a.m. flight. However, they soon learned that the airport was fogged in. For nearly twelve hours they listened to encouraging announcements that the fog was sure to clear soon. However, it never did.

At nearly 10:00 p.m., two missionary elders arrived at the airport and told them that there was a train leaving Munich for Berlin at midnight. They took Elder Packer and the others to the train station and helped them purchase their tickets for Berlin and made sure they boarded the train. As the train was pulling out, one young elder asked Elder Packer if he had any German money, to which he answered no. This young missionary was now running alongside the now-moving train. He yelled, "You better have some," and pulled a twenty-mark note from his pocket and handed it to him just as the train was pulling away.

Elder Packer explained that, back then, the Iron Curtain was very "iron." When the train stopped at Hof on the border between West Germany and East Germany, the West German crew members got off the train, and the East German crew boarded. Then the train proceeded across East Germany toward Berlin. Five-year passports were just beginning to be issued by the U.S. government at the time and Elder Packer had one. Before their trip, they tried to get his wife's passport renewed as well. However, it was sent back to them, and they were told that her three-year passport still had two more years left on it and was being honored as a five-year passport.

Around two o'clock in the morning, a stern, surly, military-type soldier who served as a conductor on the train came by for their tickets. Seeing that the Packers were not German, he told them that he needed their passports as well. Elder Packer had learned to be very careful about giving up his passport to anyone. He was especially hesitant in doing so in "unfriendly places." But, he didn't have a choice. The man simply took them from them.

The conductor returned and Elder Packer could tell that he was denying his wife's passport. The conductor left and returned a couple more times. Finally, not knowing what to do, Elder Packer had what he called "a bit of inspiration." He reached into his pocket and grabbed the twenty-mark note that the young missionary had handed to him earlier as the train was pulling away. He handed the note to the conductor, who paused only momentarily before taking the note and handing their passports back to them and walking away.

The next morning, upon arriving in Berlin, a member of the Church met them at the train. Elder Packer casually told him of their "interesting" experience with the conductor on the train. When the man heard the story, he showed a very serious look. Elder Packer asked him what was wrong. The man replied that he couldn't explain how his wife had managed to get there. He said that East Germany was the one country in the world that simply would not accept the three-year passport. In their eyes, Sister Packer did not have a passport.

Elder Packer asked, "Well, what could they have done?"

He answered, "Put you off the train."

Elder Packer said, "They wouldn't put us off the train, would they?"

The member explained that they wouldn't have put them both off the train. They would have put her (Sister Packer) off the train (at 2:00 in the morning, somewhere out in the middle of nowhere in East Germany). Elder Packer's mind reeled as he began to imagine what would have happened if they had, indeed, done this to his wife and how he would have responded. At the time that it happened, he didn't realize the serious danger they were in. People were commonly arrested and detained if their passports were not accepted by the East German authorities.

Elder Packer then pointed out that the young elder serving in the South German Mission who had handed him the twenty-mark note was a missionary from San Leandro, California, by the name of David A. Bednar (currently serving as a member of the Quorum of the Twelve Apostles). At the time, there's no way Elder Bednar could have known the consequences of his action, but it is clear that he was acting on inspiration. That twenty-mark note was worth about six dollars, which was a considerable amount for a young missionary in those days. Yet, Elder Bednar didn't hesitate. He simply (and quickly) acted on his prompting.

Elder Packer ends his story with this: "As you go through life, you will find that these things happen when you are living as you ought to live."[6]

Some "Monson Miracle" Stories

We've already talked about the fact that President Thomas S. Monson was one of the best at always acting on promptings. Many times, he didn't get to see how the story ended. And, of course, there were multiple stories where the prompting didn't really make sense or was seemingly a very small thing. But he had developed the habit to always act, so he didn't worry if the promptings didn't make any sense or if they were small. He continued forward regardless, not allowing anything or anyone to stop him from acting on the promptings he received. Not only would he act on them, but he would also do so immediately. These next three stories were shared by him in three different general conference addresses.

The Birthday Visit

> As a bishop, I worried about any members who were inactive, not attending, not serving. Such was my thought as I drove down the street where Ben and Emily lived. They were older—even in the twilight period of life. Aches and pains of advancing years caused them to withdraw from activity to the shelter of their home—isolated, detached, shut out from the mainstream of daily life and association.
>
> ***I felt the unmistakable prompting to park my car and visit Ben and Emily***, even though I was on the way to a meeting. It was a sunny weekday afternoon. I approached the door to their home and knocked. Emily answered. When she recognized me, her bishop, she exclaimed, "All day long I

6. Packer, "20–Mark Note," 2–4; emphasis added.

have waited for my phone to ring. It has been silent. I hoped that the postman would deliver a letter. He brought only bills. *Bishop, how did you know today was my birthday?*"

I answered, "**God knows, Emily, for He loves you**."

In the quiet of the living room, I said to Ben and Emily, "I don't know why I was directed here today, but our Heavenly Father knows. Let's kneel in prayer and ask Him why." This we did, and the answer came. Emily was asked to sing in the choir—even to provide a solo for the forthcoming ward conference. Ben was asked to speak to the Aaronic Priesthood young men and recount a special experience in his life when his safety was assured by responding to the promptings of the Spirit. She sang. He spoke. Hearts were gladdened by the return to activity of Ben and Emily. They rarely missed a sacrament meeting from that day to the time each was called home. ***The language of the Spirit had been spoken. It had been heard. It had been understood. Hearts were touched and lives saved***.[7]

Prompted to Check on the Woman in the Other Bed

Long years ago, when I served as a bishop, I received notification that Mary Watson, a member of my ward, was a patient in the county hospital. When I went to visit her, I discovered her in a large room with so many beds that it was difficult to single her out. As I identified her bed and approached her, I said, "Hello, Mary."

She replied, "Hello, Bishop."

I noticed that a patient in the bed next to Mary Watson covered her face with the bedsheet.

I gave Mary Watson a blessing, shook her hand, and said, "Good-bye," but I could not leave her side. *It was as though an unseen hand were resting on my shoulder*, and **I felt within my soul that I was hearing these words: "*Go over to the next bed where the little lady covered her face when you came***

7. Monson, "Spirit Giveth Life," 69; emphasis added.

in."* I did so. *I have learned in my life never to postpone a prompting.

I approached the bedside of the other patient, gently tapped her shoulder and carefully pulled back the sheet which had covered her face. Lo and behold! She, too, was a member of my ward. I had not known she was a patient in the hospital. Her name was Kathleen McKee. When her eyes met mine, she exclaimed through her tears, "Oh, Bishop, when you entered that door, I felt you had come to see me and bless me in response to my prayers. I was rejoicing inside to think that you would know I was here, but when you stopped at the other bed, my heart sank, and I knew that you had not come to see me."

I said to Kathleen McKee: "It does not matter that I didn't know you were here. It is important, however, that our Heavenly Father knew and that you had prayed silently for a priesthood blessing. ***It was He who prompted me to intrude on your privacy.***"

A blessing was given, a prayer was answered. I bestowed a kiss on her forehead and ***left the hospital with gratitude in my heart for the promptings of the Spirit.*** It would be the last time I was to see Kathleen McKee in mortality—but not the last time I heard from her.

Upon her death, the hospital called with this message: "Bishop Monson, Kathleen McKee died tonight. She made arrangements that we were to notify you, should she pass away. She left for you a key to her basement apartment."

Kathleen McKee had no immediate family. With my sweet wife accompanying me, I visited her humble apartment. I turned the key in the door, opened it, and switched on the light. There in her immaculate two-room apartment, I saw a small table with a note resting beneath an Alka-Seltzer bottle. The note, written in her own hand, said: "Bishop, my tithing is in this envelope, and the Alka-Seltzer bottle contains coins covering my fast offering. I am square with the Lord."

> The receipts were written. The sweetness of the night has not been forgotten. Tears of gratitude to God filled my very soul.[8]

Zella's Final Blessing

> On another occasion, as Sister Monson and I were driving home after visiting friends, ***I felt impressed*** **that we should go into town—a drive of many miles—to pay a visit to an elderly widow who had once lived in our ward**. Her name was Zella Thomas. At the time, she was a resident in a care center. That early afternoon we found her to be extremely frail but lying peacefully on her bed.
>
> Zella had long been blind, but she recognized our voices immediately. She asked if I might give her a blessing, adding that she was prepared to die if the Lord wanted her to return home. There was a sweet, peaceful spirit in the room, and all of us knew that her remaining time in mortality would be brief. ***Zella took me by the hand and said that she had prayed fervently that I would come to see her and provide her a blessing. I told her that we had come because of direct inspiration from our Heavenly Father.*** I kissed her on the forehead, knowing that I perhaps would not again see her in mortality. Such proved to be the case, for she passed away the following day. To have been able to provide some comfort and peace to our sweet Zella was a blessing to her and to me.[9]

Prompted to Do One Thing So God Could Use Him in a Different Way

We talked earlier about the "bank shots" that the Spirit will use to accomplish God's purposes. Here is an example of one such experience from the life of President Monson:

---

8. Monson, "Christ at Bethesda's Pool," 18–19; emphasis added.
9. Monson, 87–88; emphasis added.

One day just over a year ago, after taking care of matters at the office, ***I felt a strong impression* to visit an aged widow who was a patient at St. Joseph Villa here in Salt Lake City**. I drove there directly.

When I went to her room, I found it empty. I asked an attendant concerning her whereabouts and was directed to a lounge area. There I found this sweet widow visiting with her sister and another friend. We had a pleasant conversation together.

As we were talking, a man came to the door of the room to obtain a can of soda water from the vending machine. He glanced at me and said, "Why, you are Tom Monson."

"Yes," I replied. "And you look like a Hemingway." He acknowledged that he was Stephen Hemingway, the son of Alfred Eugene Hemingway, who had served as my counselor when I was a bishop many years ago and whom I called Gene. Stephen told me that his father was there in the same facility and was near death. He had been calling my name, and the family had wanted to contact me but had been unable to find a telephone number for me.

I excused myself immediately and went with Stephen up to the room of my former counselor, where others of his children were also gathered, his wife having passed away some years previous. **The family members regarded my meeting Stephen in the lounge area as a response by our Heavenly Father to their great desire that I would see their father before he died and answer his call. *I, too, felt that this was the case, for if Stephen had not entered the room in which I was visiting at precisely the time he did, I would not have known that Gene was even in that facility.***

We gave a blessing to him. A spirit of peace prevailed. We had a lovely visit, after which I left. The following morning a phone call revealed that Gene Hemingway had passed away—just 20 minutes after he had received the blessing from his son and me.

I expressed a silent prayer of thanks to Heavenly Father for His guiding influence which prompted my visit to St.

Joseph Villa and led me to my dear friend, Alfred Eugene Hemingway.[10]

I love how God gets involved in the tiniest of details as He blesses the lives of His sons and daughters on earth. In the story we just shared, President Monson was prompted to visit someone in the hospital. *He had a nice visit, but that wasn't why the Lord prompted him to go there.* The Lord needed him to go there so that he could be an answer to the prayers of the family of his former counselor. And then, once he got to the hospital, the Lord had to somehow get the widow to the lounge area and then get the son of his former counselor to go there as well so that he could meet up with President Monson. Yet it all came together beautifully in order for him to give that old friend a blessing just minutes before he passed away. Wow! I get goosebumps just thinking about everything that needed to happen—and how beautifully the Holy Ghost orchestrated it all.

The Bus That Was Slow to Arrive

I am the ninth of eleven children, and the eighth child is only seventeen minutes older than I am. Even though my mom was not even 5'4" tall, any mom who reads this book will be amazed to hear that my twin brother and I were delivered naturally and weighed in at exactly eighteen pounds of baby (each weighing just about nine pounds). Even more amazing, Mom still loved us after all that! Len and I are fraternal twins and have always had very different personalities and different interests, but we've also always been very close.

When we got our mission calls (on the same day), we were excited to find out that we would be serving in the same country. I served my mission as a young man in the Brazil São Paulo South Mission, while Len was serving in the Brazil Recife Mission. His mission president, Harry Eduardo Klein, had been called to open that mission for the Church. He was only twenty-nine years old when he was called to serve as mission president. Yet, when Len served there, President Klein

10. Monson, "Peace, Be Still," 55; emphasis added.

and his missionaries were the number-one baptizing mission in the Church. Both of my mission presidents told me that President Klein was one of the best missionaries that the Church had ever known. Len told me the same thing. President Klein did an outstanding job of teaching his missionaries the importance of developing and exercising faith and how to follow the promptings that would come. They followed their mission president and were blessed with miracle after miracle as they brought people into the gospel. This next story is just one of many miraculous experiences from Len's mission. It is a great example of how even *little* promptings can make a *big* difference.

One night, Len and his companion were returning home from a teaching appointment. They were at the bus stop, waiting for their bus. For some reason, the bus was taking longer than normal to arrive. Len had a thought (*Bing!*) that they should just walk home instead of continuing to wait for the bus. His senior companion told Len that it would take much longer that way. Len said, "I know, but why not? Let's just walk." Surprisingly, his companion relented and they began walking.

After a while, Len followed another *Bing!* and said to his companion, "Let's go down this road." His companion pointed out that the road Len was suggesting was not the fastest way home. Len indicated that he was aware of that, but wanted to go down that road anyway. So, they went that way.

As they were walking down that road, there was a house with its lights on. Len's third *Bing!* was to clap at that house. His companion said, "No. It is too late at night. Even if they are awake, they are probably watching TV and won't want to be interrupted." [Author's note: His companion was correct that back then, most people were tuned into their novelas, or Brazilian soap operas, late at night. They did not like to be bothered.] Len didn't accept that answer. He wanted to try. They clapped. The family answered the door and received the missionaries and their message extremely well. It was almost as if they had been waiting for them. They were truly a "golden" family. Not long after, they all joined the Church—all because a missionary followed a few different little promptings when the bus was slow to arrive. Any of those promptings would have been very easy to ignore or dismiss. Yet, many people are eternally grateful that he didn't dismiss them.

When Plan A Doesn't Work, Look for Plan C

This is another story from my younger sister, JoEllen Johnson. It is another great example of how, sometimes, the Holy Ghost will make sure that our own plan A doesn't work out so that we can be prompted to use the Lord's plan C (the celestial plan).

> It was the mid-80s. I was still a newlywed, freshly graduated from BYU, and I was called to be a Sunday School teacher for course 16–17. Back then, there wasn't a strict teaching schedule; you just picked any lesson from the manual. Typically, I would flip through the manual on Sunday night and find a lesson I wanted to teach the following Sunday so I could think about it during the week. That worked just fine until one Sunday when I couldn't land on a lesson that felt right. I tried a couple more times during the week and could never settle on one.
>
> Finally, on Saturday night, in what felt like an act of desperation, I asked my husband to come to my class and talk about his mission in Switzerland. I prepared some scriptures and quotes about missionary work to supplement his message. The lesson went well. As I was about to leave the building afterward, one of the boys in my class—one of those very active kids whom I was not even worried about—came up to me and said, "This morning I got up and looked in the mirror and thought, 'Ok, if someone teaches a lesson on missionary work today, I'll go on a mission.'"
>
> I was stunned, but I playfully put my hands on his shoulders and shook him a little while saying, "Hey! Don't put that kind of pressure on me!" But then I was curious. I went home and looked at that manual again. In that entire manual, there was not one lesson on missionary work. And then I realized—what felt to me like a last-minute scramble was really the Lord guiding me to do what He wanted me to do. That was why I could never feel right about any of the lessons during the week. And that was also why I was guided to ask my husband to come and talk about

his mission. I felt very grateful to be a part of the Lord's response to this young man.

Every day, revelation is being given to countless people across the globe. Sometimes, the prompting that we may get will be something that *seems really small and insignificant*. And we may even get *another thought that will try to confirm to us that it really is not all that important—or that we are too busy for something that small.* When that happens, we need to resist the urge to listen to that second voice and *act on every prompting from the Holy Ghost, no matter how small the act may seem*. Because, in reality, oftentimes that small act from you will be an ***important answer to someone else's prayer in their hour of need.***

CHAPTER 11

Now What?

"I know of no experience more sweet or feeling more precious than to heed a prompting only to discover that the Lord has answered another person's prayer through you."

—Thomas S. Monson[1]

Isn't it interesting that our last two prophets, Thomas S. Monson and Russell M. Nelson, have both exerted such tremendous effort to talk about the gift of the Holy Ghost and of our need to have it and use it more in our lives than we currently do? President Nelson has spoken with a great sense of urgency about our responsibilities in this regard. You recall his quote that we have shared in this book—and that you have heard countless times before: "In coming days, it will not be possible to survive spiritually without the guiding, directing, comforting, and constant influence of the Holy Ghost."[2] *There is a reason that he speaks so urgently about this.* It is my prayer that we will heed his counsel—that we will work hard to have the Spirit become our constant companion and to recognize His promptings and act on them immediately.

Before I end this book with a couple more stories, I want to share a few important reminders that I hope will help as we move forward, working to seek for and act on promptings from the Holy Ghost on a daily basis:

---

1. Monson, "Peace, Be Still," 55.
2. Nelson, "Revelation for Our Lives," 96.

Don't Beat Yourself Up about the Past

I worry that if you are not careful, your first takeaway from this book may be to beat yourself up over all the times that you listened to the second voice and, as a result, did not act on the promptings that you received from the Holy Ghost. I'm sure that each of us could easily remember many specific times in our lives where this has happened. I can recall a number of similar experiences from my life. ***Do not spend any time beating yourself up over past experiences in following the promptings of the second voice.*** It serves no good purpose. Besides, you didn't know any better. Rather than beating yourself up, use this as a new starting point for a wonderful future (like President Monson did when he arrived at the hospital too late).

Don't Think That You Will Get Revelation for the Church

Another wrong takeaway from this book would be to believe that you'll get promptings for the Church, as a whole. I doubt that this is a concern for most people. But, if we are not sufficiently humble, the adversary can try to mess with us a little bit in this regard. You will recall the story we shared earlier in this book about Hiram Page thinking he was getting revelations for the Church and Joseph Smith had to correct him. To help remove any possible doubt that someone may have on this matter, I will share a few quotes from our Church leaders:

- "It is contrary to the economy of God for any member of the Church, or any one [else], to receive instruction for those in authority, higher than themselves" (Joseph Smith).[3]
- "There is an appointed way . . . in which revelation from the Lord for the government of his church is received. *There is but one man on the earth, at a time, who holds this power*" (Wilford Woodruff).[4]
- "In these latter days, ***we affirm that only the prophet may receive revelation through the Holy Ghost for the entire Church.*** Some forget this, as when Aaron and Miriam tried to convince Moses to agree with them. But the Lord taught them

3. Smith, *Teachings of the Prophet*, 18.
4. Woodruff, *Discourses*, 54; emphasis added.

and us. He said: 'If there be a prophet among you, I the Lord will make myself known unto him. . . . With him will I speak mouth to mouth.' [Numbers 12:6, 8]" (Robert D. Hales).[5]

Don't Think That You Will Get Revelation for People Over Whom You Have No Stewardship

Similarly—and this is an area where the adversary may be a bit more likely to get someone to err—Satan will try to deceive some well-intentioned people into believing that they will get revelation for other people. Be careful. Know that ***you will not get revelation for people over whom you have no stewardship***. Don't be fooled into thinking that you will. Again, let's read what our Church leaders have said on this very subject:

- "You may receive revelation individually, as a parent for your family, or for those for whom you are responsible as a leader or teacher, having been properly called and set apart" (Boyd K. Packer).[6]
- "The right of revelation for others does not extend beyond our own stewardship" (James E. Faust).[7]
- "As we receive the inspiration of the Holy Ghost for ourselves, it is wise to remember that we cannot receive revelation for others. I know of a young man who told a young woman, 'I've had a dream that you are to be my wife.' The young woman pondered that statement and then responded, 'When I have the same dream, I'll come and talk to you'" (Robert D. Hales).[8]

Don't Think You Are Bad or Something Is Wrong with You if You Are Getting Promptings from the Adversary

I know we spoke of this earlier, but it is important enough to repeat. When you get those promptings from the adversary, don't let him make you think there is something wrong with you. Instead,

---

5. Hales, "Holy Ghost," 105–106; emphasis added.
6. Packer, "Personal Revelation," 61.
7. Faust, "Communion," 4.
8. Hales, "Holy Ghost," 106.

congratulations! You are in great company. It happened to Jesus Christ. It happened to Moses. It happened to Joseph Smith. And now, it's happening to you. Instead of believing that there is something wrong with you, you should look at it in just the opposite manner. It means that Satan is trying to throw you off track before you do something great. Just hang in there. It is highly likely that something awesome and very spiritual is about to happen (and that is why the adversary is trying so hard to mess with you to keep it from happening).

Don't Give Up When It doesn't Seem to Work Out the First Few Times That You Try to Follow a Prompting!

Remember, when you first start making efforts to diligently follow the promptings of the Holy Ghost, the adversary will do everything in his power to get you to stop doing so. He knows even better than you do what a powerful gift the Holy Ghost is. That is why he works so hard to do the following:

- Get you to not be worthy to have the Holy Ghost as your companion.
- Cause you to doubt that a prompting really was from the Holy Ghost.
- Convince you that his (Satan's) promptings are really your own thoughts.
- Make it seem that things "didn't work out" when you try to follow a prompting so that you will believe that it wasn't really a prompting from the Holy Ghost—it was just your own thought—and, as a result, not follow future promptings you will get.

When these things happen, you have to be strong and push through the feelings that the adversary wants you to have. If he can get you to give up and quit on this quest early on, he will win on the hundreds of promptings that you won't follow in the future. So he may call in reinforcements early on to "double down" against you and get you to stop trying and even stop believing that those were really promptings from the Holy Ghost. Why? Because he knows that, most times, it only takes a little bit of discouragement early on to get good people to give up. Do not be that kind of a person. Be committed.

If it really is the greatest gift that can be bestowed upon us—***and it is***—then it is worth fighting for. Keep at it!

Don't Let Satan's Distractions Keep You from Hearing and Recognizing the Promptings from the Holy Ghost

The adversary uses many numerous distractions with us. Be aware that this number will only continue to grow. The adversary will use anything and everything he can to keep our focus away from the Spirit and on to the newest "shiny thing" that will keep our attention away from God. Be very careful. Give yourself time every single day—a time for just you and God—to sit in a quiet place and meditate and pray.

Reminder of Five Facts about the Adversary's Promptings

Although we spent a good amount of time in an earlier chapter going into more detail about each of these five important facts to remember about the promptings from the adversary, they are so important that I felt we should list them one more time to remind you of each of these important facts to end the book. He does not want you to remember these facts about him and his promptings. He is counting on you falling for them again and again. So, as a reminder, the five things to remember are:

1. Satan won't prompt you to do good.
2. Satan is usually the second voice (or second prompting).
3. Satan uses great logic with his promptings.
4. Satan wants you to believe that his promptings are your own thoughts.
5. Satan oftentimes will speak to you in the first person.

I hope you will remember these facts and not allow the adversary to fool you any longer. He has had far too much success with all of us. Information is power. Now that we know this information about him, let's turn it into a power that will keep us from being susceptible to his tricks.

Are You Living Far Beneath Your Privileges?

Having the Holy Ghost as our companion and not using Him as a revelator in our lives is kind of like being given a brand-new private jet as a gift and then just putting it on a trailer and towing it around everywhere we want to go. People would wonder why we have it. What a waste. That is what it is like to have this amazing gift and not use it the way it was meant to be used in our lives.

Perhaps a better analogy is the cell phone. Cell phones these days can do just about anything you want them to do. Yet many people in the older generation use a cell phone pretty much only as a phone and never take advantage of so many other things that their phone can do for them. If, similarly, we are using the Holy Ghost only to feel good when we hear a spiritual story or a great talk, we are wasting the greatest gift that can be bestowed upon us.

Brigham Young spoke very clearly about this point when he said, "There is no doubt, if a person lives according to the revelations given to God's people, he may have the Spirit of the Lord to signify to him His will, and to ***guide and to direct him in the discharge of his duties, in his temporal as well as his spiritual exercises. I am satisfied, however, that in this respect, we live far beneath our privileges.***"[9]

In this book, we have talked about the importance of trusting in those positive thoughts to say or do something good. We talked about how we need to avoid listening to that second voice and, instead, act immediately on that first prompting. We pointed out that, even if it doesn't make sense, we should still act on the prompting right away. We also came to the realization that even when it seems like a very small, unimportant thing, it usually won't be a small thing to the other person. We just need to commit to act!

Michelle D. Craig said,

> ***Get your errand from the Lord. The prayer Heavenly Father seems eager to answer is our plea to be led to someone who needs our help***. President Henry B. Eyring has taught us to seek revelation by asking God who we can help for Him. "*If you ask*

9. Young, *Journal of Discourses*, 12:104; emphasis added.

questions like that, the Holy Ghost will come and you'll feel nudges about things you can do for other people. When you go and do those things, you're on the Lord's errand, and ***when you're on the Lord's errand, you qualify for the gift of the Holy Ghost.***"

You can pray and ask the Lord for an errand. As you do, ***He can use your ordinary skills to accomplish His extraordinary work.***[10]

God Is in Charge

Before I share one final story from the life of President Thomas S. Monson, I want to point out that although President Monson was great at following promptings of the Holy Ghost, it wasn't because he was the Prophet of God. Rather, it was because of his commitment to seek promptings and to act on them immediately when they came to him. You will note that many of the stories I have shared about him in this book occurred when he was a young bishop. It is a commitment that he kept for most of his life. It is my prayer that we will do the same.

I will try to summarize this wonderful story about President Monson that was shared by Elder Jeffrey R. Holland in the February 1986 *Ensign.* It illustrates how God really is in charge and will orchestrate things the way He wants. We just need to be willing to do our part (as President Monson was always doing his):

One weekend in August 1974, Elder Thomas S. Monson received a last-minute change of assignment that sent him to the Shreveport Louisiana Stake. When he arrived, he found the Saturday afternoon schedule to be packed with meetings. The stake president knew that there wasn't time for it, but he asked Elder Monson if it would be possible for him to give a blessing to a ten-year-old cancer patient from his stake by the name of Christal Methvin. Elder Monson replied that he would be happy to do so. With the tight timeline, he hoped she would be attending the conference, but knew there was a chance that she was in a nearby hospital. The stake president informed him that, sadly, Christal was confined to her home, which was many miles away from Shreveport. Upon a closer look at the meeting schedule, Elder

10. Craig, "Spiritual Capacity," 19–20; emphasis added.

Monson saw that there was simply no time available for such a visit. He suggested that, instead, they would have every person praying in each of the sessions of conference remember Christal in their prayers. He was sure that the Lord would understand and He would bless Crystal and the Methvin family.

Elder Monson was unaware of what had happened prior to this conference. Christal had lost her leg to surgery. Unfortunately, after the surgery, they discovered that the cancer had already spread to the lungs of this poor little girl. The family then planned a trip to Salt Lake City, where they hoped Christal would be able to receive a blessing from one of the General Authorities. Since the Methvins did not know any of the Brethren personally, they showed Christal a picture of all the leaders of the Church. As they did so, she pointed to the photo of Elder Monson and said that she wanted him to be the one to give her a blessing.

Unfortunately, Christal's condition had worsened so quickly that they ended up having to cancel the planned flight to Salt Lake. Her body was quickly growing weaker, but her faith seemed to be *growing* just as fast. She told her family, "Since a General Authority is coming to our stake conference, why not Brother Monson? If I can't go to him, the Lord can send him to me." It was about at this same time that Elder Monson received an unexpected change in his stake conference assignment for that weekend. He would now be going to the Shreveport stake.

The whole family was overjoyed when they learned that Elder Monson was, indeed, going to be the General Authority coming to their stake conference. United in faith and their love for Christal, the family knelt by her bedside to ask for just one more blessing: They prayed that Christal would receive a personal visit from Elder Monson. Later, they received a call from the stake president, explaining that the meeting schedule was just too tight and, as a result, Elder Monson would not be able to visit Christal as he had hoped. The family decided to kneel around Christal's bed one more time. They pleaded for a final favor on behalf of their suffering little angel daughter and sister: that somehow, she would yet be able to receive a blessing from Elder Monson.

At the very moment that the Methvin family was gathered around Christal's bed, offering their humble plea to the Lord, Elder Monson was looking over his notes, preparing to give the concluding remarks for the Saturday evening session of conference. He was walking to the pulpit when he got an impression so strong that he says it was nearly audible. What was the message that overpowered him? "Suffer the little children to come unto me, and forbid them not: for of such is the kingdom of God."

With that strong message received, his notes became a blur. The name and image of Christal Methvin remained in the forefront of his mind, making it nearly impossible for him to follow the outlined theme of the meeting. So, he stopped and acted upon the message from the Spirit that he received. He announced changes to the next day's conference schedule. He knew it would cause a lot of disruption and even confusion among the stake's members. But, those changes needed to be made because there was a little girl who he needed to visit the next morning. Once those changes were made for the next day, he allowed the meeting to continue.

Early Sunday morning, Elder Monson drove the many miles to the Methvin home. When he arrived, he was led into the room where Christal lay. This beautiful little girl was now too ill to rise and too weak to speak. She was also now blind as a result of her cruel illness. Elder Monson fell to his knees. He was overcome by what he saw and even more by the Spirit of the Lord that was so strong in this home. He gently took Christal's hand in his and whispered to her, "Christal . . . I am here!" It took a great deal of effort, but this sweet little daughter of God, showing her great faith, replied back softly, "Brother Monson, I just knew you would come."

Elder Monson then pronounced a blessing in which he commended Christal's body and spirit to the loving watchcare of her Heavenly Father. He knew that God was observing all that was occurring in this home at that time. When he concluded, little Chrystal said, "Thank you." It was barely audible but seemed to be a perfect benediction to not only the blessing that had just occurred but also to the short and faith-filled life she had led.

The following Thursday, Elder Monson made sure that little Christal was remembered in the prayer circle of the First Presidency and Council of the Twelve Apostles. While this was happening in Salt Lake City, many miles away in the Methvin home, little Chrystal's pure spirit was finally freed from her disease-ravaged body and she was warmly welcomed into the paradise of God.[11]

---

11. Holland, "President Thomas S. Monson," 15–16; emphasis added.

Moving Forward

With a desire to be a spiritual first responder on a daily basis, let us remember how God responds as He watches over us. I love what President Spencer W. Kimball told us: "God does notice us, and He watches over us. **But it is usually through another person that He meets our needs**."[12]

President Ezra Taft Benson said something similar in a different way, but it is also an important message and the perfect summary of this book: "The great task of life is to **learn the will of the Lord and then do it.**"[13]

In fact, in Revelation 3:20, the Lord has told us that He has done His part and now it is up to us. He says, "Behold, I stand at the door, and knock: if any man hear my voice, and open the door, I will come in to him, and will sup with him, and he with me." In this scripture, I hope you can hear the Lord telling you that He is *always* trying to communicate to us. It is up to us to open the door—to live worthily and to pray for His promptings and to be on alert for every prompting from the Holy Ghost that comes our way. There is no question—He *is knocking all of the time.* Let's answer the door!

Start Your Day the Right Way

Although I shared this quote from Elder Rasband in chapter 4, it is such a great summary of the message of this book that I want to reiterate it: "The Lord knows the needs of all His children—and He knows who is prepared to help. **If we let the Lord know in our morning prayers that we are ready, He will call on us to respond**. If we respond, He will call on us time and time again and we will find ourselves on what President Monson calls 'the Lord's errand.' **We will become spiritual first responders bringing help from on high**."[14] We need to commit to start *every day* with this as a part of our morning prayer.

---

12. Kimball, "Small Acts of Service," 5; emphasis added.
13. Benson, "Great Commandment," 4.
14. Rasband, "Let the Holy Spirit Guide," 96; emphasis added.

Start Creating—and Saving—Your Own Miracle Stories

It is my prayer that, as you finish reading this book, you will decide to sign up today to be one of God's spiritual first responders and start your day with that one request in your morning prayers. Ask God to trust you with at least one prompting that day—and promise Him that you will act on it as soon as it comes. As you do this, you will start recognizing more *Bings!* than ever before, because God needs us to help in His work. And, as you act on them, you will help bless many of God's children. As an added bonus, every so often, you may even get to know "the rest of the story"!

As you start having these experiences, I hope you will record them. If you are already a journal writer, that is great. Just add these wonderful stories to them. If you are not a journal writer, I hope you will decide to start being one, at least to document the *Bings!* that come to you and what happens as you act on them.

Even as you have been reading this book, you have had some promptings. I hope that, when they came, you put the book down and acted on them. You can always come back and pick the book back up and continue reading, but many times the prompting you get may be the only chance you will get to help that person. Don't miss out. Act *immediately*! If you are having a *Bing*! moment right now, what are you doing still reading this book? **Put the book down and go act!**

Remember—God Wants to Communicate with You!

Yes . . . God *wants* to talk to us. We already quoted from Doctrine and Covenants 121:33, which says: "What power shall stay the heavens? As well might man stretch forth his puny arm to stop the Missouri river in its decreed course, or to turn it up stream, as to hinder the Almighty from pouring down knowledge from heaven upon the heads of the Latter-day Saints."

In Doctrine and Covenants 42:61, the Lord says further, "If thou shalt ask, thou shalt receive revelation upon revelation, knowledge upon knowledge, that thou mayest know the mysteries and peaceable things—that which bringeth joy, that which bringeth life eternal."

What if we have been reading too much into that verse? I'm sure that most people probably think that the Lord is talking about some grand revelation. But what if God is talking about the kind of revelations that we have been discussing in this book? We would need to know His "mysteries"—such as whom to call and what to say—in order to bless the lives of others. And those "mysteries" would definitely be the "peaceable things." They would bring joy—to us *and* to those we help—and in many cases, they will bring eternal life to those whom the Lord directs us to help.

We need to remember what we learned from Alma's teaching to his son Helaman in Alma 37:6–7 in the Book of Mormon: many times, it is by small and simple things that great things are brought to pass.

Let's not make it more complicated than it needs to be. President Monson and President Nelson have taught us this very principle—both in word and in deed. Let's do as God taught us through Alma's words and "keep it simple." Let's recognize those positive thoughts to say something or do something as promptings from the Holy Ghost, and let's act on them immediately, no matter how small and insignificant they may seem.

I Would Love to Hear from You!

As you begin your journey of focusing on the *Bings!* that you are getting on a regular basis and acting on those positive thoughts to say or do something, I would love to hear from you. If you have some of your own personal experiences with *Bings!*—either ones where you followed them or ones where you didn't but wish you had—that you feel comfortable sharing with me, I invite you to email me at loren@HeavensBings.com. As you share your personal stories with me, let me know if you want them to remain only between you and me or if you feel comfortable in having me consider using your story in a future book about *Bings!* to help inspire others.

With many people sharing their stories with me, I worry that I may not be able to respond personally to each email that I receive. But I hope that each of us will continue to seek for and act on the *Bings!* that we get from the Holy Ghost—especially now that we all know how to recognize them. This is what God wants. I am excited to have us all join together with Him in changing the lives of those around us—sometimes in small ways and, at other times, in big ways.

Don't forget, most of the time, it may appear that when you acted on your prompting, "it didn't work out." Don't let that slow you down! Just shrug your shoulders and smile—knowing that you did what God wanted—and move forward.

Don't Give Ultimatums to God

I love the following story, but every time I share it, I worry that someone will have the wrong takeaway from it. In order to avoid that this time, let me address it head on. **Do not ever** think it is a good idea for you to "test God" or give Him an ultimatum (as the woman in this upcoming story did). I repeat: Don't ever give ultimatums to God! When you do something like that—telling Him that, unless He makes some miracle occur, you are going to do something extraordinarily stupid like leave the Church or, even worse, take your life—you are taking a big gamble.

Let me explain why that is such a terrible idea: What if the person that the Holy Ghost prompts to step in and do what you need at that time chooses *not* to act on the prompting that he or she receives? Now that you have learned about how many people listen to the second prompting and end up not acting on the first prompting, I hope this will be enough to convince you to never give God an ultimatum. You don't ever want to put yourself in that position. Since we know that many people don't act on their promptings, giving God an ultimatum is a *terrible* idea. It is a form of the worst kind of gambling in which you could ever take part!

Instead, the point that you should take away from this next story is that you want to be one of those spiritual first responders that Elder Rasband told us about. Commit to begin your days, in your morning prayers every day, asking God to trust you with at least one prompting that day—and promise Him you will act on it the very minute that it comes. We should want to be one of those people who constantly impact the lives of others for good because of their closeness to the Spirit.

A Simple Phone Call Saved a Life

Of all of the people I have known personally in my life, my mother was by far the person closest to the Spirit. It was amazing how easily she felt and acted on promptings of the Spirit. She had tuned her "celestial radio" in extremely well. She taught us in a family home evening once about how, every day, in her personal morning prayers, she asked Heavenly Father to trust her with at least one prompting that day. And then she promised Him that she would act immediately on every prompting that she received. As a result, she saw miracles daily. But she said that most of the time, she would act on her promptings and things didn't seem to go well. However, she learned to never doubt and to just keep acting on her promptings, trusting that God knew what He was doing by asking her to do these things. She realized that she did not need to know the "rest of the story." If it didn't seem to work out as she had hoped, she just smiled, shrugged her shoulders, and returned to whatever she had been doing prior to receiving the prompting.

In that same family home evening lesson, she shared a beautiful story with us. At first, her efforts to help someone didn't seem to go well, but later she did get to hear "the rest of the story." She told us that this story had happened years earlier and, of course, she didn't share with us the name of the woman. But it went like this: One day, my mom was doing laundry [*Author's note:* Since I am number nine of eleven kids, my poor mother was *always* doing laundry]. Anyway, while she was doing laundry, she got the impression (*Bing!*) that she needed to call a woman in the ward. So, because of her commitment to *act immediately on every prompting*, she put the laundry down and went to the phone and made the call. The conversation went something like this:

Other Woman: "Hello" (in a mean, irritated voice).
My Mom: "Hi! This is Sister Dalton. How are you doing?"
Other Woman: (in that same mean voice) "Fine."
My Mom: "Well, I just had a feeling that I should call you!"
Other Woman: "Okay" (not sounding any happier).
My Mom: "Is there anything I can do for you?"
Other Woman: "No. Bye!" (angrily hangs up the phone)

Even though the conversation went as it did, my mom—because she had learned to never doubt her promptings—amazingly stayed in good spirits and just shrugged her shoulders, smiled, and went back to folding laundry. She told us that she had taught herself to know in situations like this that she had done what God wanted her to do—and that the rest was up to God and the person she reached out to help by acting on her prompting. Typically, this would be the end of the story (at least that is how many of her stories ended, with her just trusting in God that what He wanted to have done had been done). But, in this case, she got to hear a little bit about "the rest of the story."

Three days later, a knock came at our door, and Mom answered it. It was the woman she had called three days earlier. In that same irritated voice, she asked Mom, "Why did you call me the other day?"

Mom replied, "I just felt that I needed to call you."

The woman did not accept that answer. She seemed to get even more upset and said, "No. I need to know. Three days ago, *why did you call me right when you did*?"

My mom lovingly said, "If you want to come in and sit down, I will share with you why." After they both sat down, Mom said, "It was kind of interesting. I was folding the laundry, and all of a sudden I got a strong feeling that I needed to call you right then. So I stopped doing the laundry, and I went to the phone and called you. I'm sorry. It was obvious that I caught you at a bad time, and I am sorry for that." With that, the woman started to sob uncontrollably. Mom put her arm around her and just let her cry.

Finally, when the woman gained her composure, she said, "No. Let me tell *you* why you called me! I had been falling into a deeper state of depression for weeks—probably more like months. It seemed that life just kept getting worse and worse for me. I kept it hidden from everyone as best I could. But three days ago, I had finally reached my limit. I decided that I was going to kill myself. I got on my knees and said a prayer to God and told Him that unless a miracle happened, my sweet husband would be coming home to a dead wife that night. I got up from the prayer—and was in the very act, itself—when the phone rang. It startled me so much that, without even thinking, I answered the phone. As soon as I answered it, I said to myself, 'Why did I answer the phone?' That was why I was so rude to you, and I am sorry that I was.

"As soon as I hung up the phone, a thought popped into my head. [*Author's note:* By now, you know that her thought was a *Bing!*]That thought said, 'That was your miracle.' I kept trying to tell myself that it was just a stupid coincidence. In fact, it was worse than a coincidence; it was an *annoyance*! But every time I tried to say that, the thought came back to me [*Bing!*], 'No. That was your miracle. Go ask her.' I kept hoping that the thought would leave, but for three days, it has stayed with me. So I finally had to come and ask you. And ***now I know that God not only knows who I am, but that He loves me. Thank you so much for acting on that prompting, Sister Dalton***. I know that to you, it probably seemed like a very small, insignificant thing. I could easily understand if you decided not to call me. But you need to know that your simple phone call to me *saved my life*!"

After Mom shared this story with us, she asked us a question that has stayed with me ever since that FHE lesson: "What would have happened if—when I got that prompting to call her—I had said, 'I will call her . . . after I finish doing the laundry'?"

As I stated earlier, not only do we need to act on our first promptings—our *Bings!*—but we also need to train ourselves to act on them immediately—as soon as we get them!

Will You Be a Spiritual First Responder?

Not only does God want to talk to us, but He also wants to bless His children's lives. He is looking for more willing participants who want to be part of His army—His spiritual first responders—and be tools in His hand. Sign up today! You'll be glad you did. In fact, you won't be the only one who will be glad you did; so will all of the people whose lives you will touch. Additionally, many of their ancestors and descendants will be eternally grateful that you acted on your promptings.

To put it as simply as possible, let's just follow the counsel of President Thomas S. Monson: "**Do not postpone a prompting; rather, act on it, and the Lord will open the way**."[15]

---

15. Monson," Sacred Call of Service," 55; emphasis added.

I'd like to end this book with what Steven L. Brown used to say to me. Steve was my first counselor when I served as the bishop of the Hidden Lake Ward in the Tracy California Stake, and he has been a dear friend ever since. As we served together, he often would say the following phrase just before we set out doing things like leading a meeting or going to visit people. Some readers may already be familiar with the saying, but it's a great thought that can serve as a sweet reminder to all of us about our daily responsibility here on earth—and it's how I would like to finish this book: "Now let's go out there and give 'em Heaven!"

BIBLIOGRAPHY

Anderson, Jared, "Acting on Spiritual Promptings," BYU—Hawaii devotional, October 3, 2018, https://speeches.byuh.edu/devotional/acting-on-spiritual-promptings.

Anderson, Neil L. "Beware of the Evil behind the Smiling Eyes," *Ensign*, May 2005, 46–48.

Ballard, M. Russell. "Now Is the Time," *Ensign*, October 2000, 75–77.

Beck, Julie B. "And upon the Handmaids in Those Days Will I Pour Out My Spirit," *Ensign*, May 2010, 10–12.

Bednar, David A. "An Evening with a General Authority—Elder Bednar Discussion." Interview by Chad Webb, *Gospel Media*, The Church of Jesus Christ of Latter-day Saints, February 2020. Video, 1:01:28, https://www.churchofjesuschrist.org/media/video/2020-02-1020-an-evening-with-a-general-authority-elder-bednar-discussion?lang=eng&collectionId=a43e55b417da4f2e942eba0456cc1e26.

Bednar, David A. "Receive the Holy Ghost," *Ensign*, November 2010, 94–97.

Bednar, David A. "Receiving, Recognizing, and Responding to the Promptings of the Holy Ghost," Devotionals and Speeches, BYU—Idaho, August 31, 1999, https://www.byui.edu/devotionals/president-david-a-bednar-devotional-summer-1999.

Bednar, David A. "The Spirit of Revelation," *Ensign*, May 2011, 87–90.

Bednar, David A. "That We May Always Have His Spirit to Be with Us," *Ensign*, May 2006, 28–31.

Bennett, Archibald F. *Saviors on Mount Zion*. Salt Lake City, UT: Deseret Sunday School Union Board, 1950.

Benson, Ezra Taft. "The Great Commandment—Love the Lord," *Ensign*, May 1988, 4–6.

Benson, Ezra Taft. "Seek the Spirit of the Lord," *Ensign*, April 1988, 2–5.

Bergera, Gary James, compiler. *Statements of the LDS First Presidency: A Topical Compendium*. Salt Lake City, UT: Signature Books, 2007.

Bigler, Henry W., contributor. "Recollections of the Prophet Joseph Smith," *The Juvenile Instructor*, March 1, 1892.

"Birthday Lasagna," *Ensign*, August 2019, 66.

"Church Honors Missionaries Who Died in South America." In "News of the Church," *Ensign*, August 1989, 74.

Christensen, Clayton M. *The Power of Everyday Missionaries: The What and How of Sharing the Gospel.* Salt Lake City, UT: Deseret Book, 2012.

Christensen, Craig C. "An Unspeakable Gift from God," *Ensign*, November 2012, 12–15.

Christiansen, ElRay L. "Can Satan or his hosts read our thoughts, and do they still have a knowledge of our pre-earth life, which would and could aid them in tempting us?" In "Questions and Answers," *Ensign*, July 1975, 49.

Christofferson, D. Todd. "When Thou Art Converted," *Ensign*, May 2004, 11–13.

Clark, James R., compiler. *Messages of the First Presidency of The Church of Jesus Christ of Latter-day Saints.* 6 vols. Salt Lake City, UT: Bookcraft, 1965–76.

Cook, Gene R. "Spiritual Guides for Teachers of Righteousness," *Ensign*, May 1982, 25–27.

Covey, Stephen R. "Put First Things First." In *7 Habits of Highly Effective People*, 145–182. New York: Free Press, 2004. First published in 1989 by Simon and Schuster (New York).

Craig, Michelle D. "Divine Discontent," *Ensign*, November 2018, 52–55.

Craig, Michelle D. "Spiritual Capacity," *Ensign*, November 2019, 19–21.

Durham, Mary R. "A Child's Guiding Gift," *Ensign*, May 2016, 23–25.

Edgley, Richard C. "Satan's Bag of Snipes," *Ensign*, November 2000, 42–43.

Eyring, Henry B. "The Holy Ghost as Your Companion," *Ensign*, November 2015, 104–107.

Eyring, Henry B. "We Are One," *Ensign*, May 2013, 62–65.

Faulkner, Garnee, "Fresh Crab and French Bread." In "Mormon Journal," *Ensign*, June 1985, 38–39.

Faust, James E. "Communion with the Holy Spirit," *Ensign*, March 2002, 3–7.

Faust, James E. "The Gift of the Holy Ghost—A Sure Compass," *Ensign*, May 1989, 31–33.

Faust, James E. "The Great Imitator," *Ensign*, November 1987, 33–36.

Faust, James E. "The Voice of the Spirit," Speeches, BYU, September 5, 1993, https://speeches.byu.edu/talks/james-e-faust/voice-spirit.

Gale, Blaine L. "Speaking Words I Didn't Understand." In "Spiritual Promptings," *Ensign*, September 2008, 18–19.

Godoy, Carlos. A. "I Believe in Angels," *Engsin*, November 2020, 86–88.

Grant, Heber J. *Gospel Standards: Selections from the Sermons and Writings of Heber J. Grant, Seventh President of the Church of Jesus Christ of Latter-day Saints.* Compiled by G. Homer Durham under the direction of John A. Widtsoe and Richard L. Evans. 7th ed. *Improvement Era*, 1943.

Hales, Robert D. "The Holy Ghost," *Ensign*, May 2016, 105–107.

Hallstrom, Donald L. "I *Am* a Child of God," *Ensign*, May 2016, 26–28.

Halverson, Taylor and Doug Witney, "2 Things Distracting Us from Hearing the Voice of God in Our Lives + How to Tune Them Out," *LDS Living*, October 24, 2017, https://www.ldsliving.com/2-Things-Distracting-Us-from-Hearing-the-Voice-of-God-in-Our-Lives-How-to-Tune-Them-Out/s/86760.

Hardy, David J. "Warned in a Dream," *Liahona*, February 1986, https://abn.churchofjesuschrist.org/study/liahona/1986/02/warned-in-a-dream?lang=eng.

Hinckley, Gordon B. *Teachings of Gordon B. Hinckley*. Salt Lake City, UT: Deseret Book, 1997.

Holland, Jeffrey R. "Be With and Strengthen Them," *Ensign*, May 2018, 101–103.

Holland, Jeffrey R. "Cast Not Away Therefore Your Confidence," Speeches, BYU, March 2, 1999, https://speeches.byu.edu/talks/jeffrey-r-holland/cast-not-away-therefore-your-confidence.

Holland, Jeffrey R. "The Ministry of Angels," *Ensign*, November 2008, 29–31.

Holland, Jeffrey R. "President Thomas S. Monson: Man of Action, Man of Faith, Always 'on the Lord's Errand,'" *Ensign*, February 1986, 11–17.

Johnson, Peter M. "Power to Overcome the Adversary," *Ensign*, November 2019, 110–112.

Kendrick, L. Lionel, "Personal Revelation," Speeches, BYU, May 20, 1997, https://speeches.byu.edu/talks/l-lionel-kendrick/personal-revelation.

Kimball, Spencer W. *Faith Precedes the Miracle*. Salt Lake City, UT: Deseret, 1977.

Kimball, Spencer W. *The Miracle of Forgiveness*. Salt Lake City, UT: Bookcraft, 1969.

Kimball, Spencer W. "My brothers and sisters and friends the world over, we bring you greeting . . ." Conference Report, April 1964 (134th Annual Conference), 93–99.

Kimball, Spencer W. "Small Acts of Service," *Ensign*, December 1974, 2–7.

Kimball, Spencer W. *The Teachings of Spencer W. Kimball*. Ed. Edward L. Kimball. Salt Lake City, UT: Deseret Book, 2002. First published 1982 by Bookcraft (Salt Lake City, UT).

Kimball, Spencer W. "The Things of Eternity—Stand We in Jeopardy?" *Ensign*, January 1977, 3–7.

Lee, Harold B. *Stand ye in Holy Places: Selected sermons and writings of President Harold B. Lee*. Salt Lake City, UT: Deseret Book, 1976. First published 1974.

Lee, Harold B. "Stories from the General Authorities: President Harold B. Lee," *New Era*, March 1973, 9–12.

Lee, Harold B. "When Your Heart Tells You Things Your Mind Does Not Know," *New Era*, February 1971, 2–4.

Lay, KaRyn. "To the Rescue." Produced by KaRyn Lay and Sarah Blake. *This is the Gospel*, June 17, 2019. Podcast, episode 30. https://www.ldsliving.com/pages/this-is-the-gospel-e30-to-the-rescue.

Lewis, C.S. *Mere Christianity*. New York: HarperOne, 2001. First published 1952 by Geoffrey Bles (London, UK).

Limb, Gordon, "Recognizing and Responding to the Promptings of the Spirit," Speeches, BYU, March 5, 2013, https://speeches.byu.edu/talks/gordon-limb/recognizing-and-responding-to-the-promptings-of-the.

Loski, Diana. "A Mother's Intuition." In "Spiritual Promptings," *Ensign*, September 2008, 22.

Lyon, Jack M. Linda Ririe Gunry, Jay A. Parry, and Devan Jensen, eds. *Best-Loved Poems of the LDS People*. Salt Lake City, UT: Deseret Book, 1996.

Madsen, Truman G. *Joseph Smith the Prophet*. Salt Lake City, UT: Bookcraft, 1989.

Markham, Edwin. *Poems of Edwin Markham*. Selected and arranged by Charles L. Wallis. New York: Harper & Brothers, 1950.

Maxwell, Neal A. "Meek and Lowly," Speeches, *BYU*, October 21, 1986, https://speeches.byu.edu/talks/neal-a-maxwell/meek-lowly.

Maxwell, Neal A. *The Promise of Discipleship*. Salt Lake City, UT: Deseret Book, 2010. First published 2001.

Millet, Robert L. *The Holy Spirit: His Identity, Mission, and Ministry*. Salt Lake City, UT: Deseret Book, 2019.

Monson, Thomas S. "Christ at Bethesda's Pool," *Ensign*, November 1996, 16–19.

Monson, Thomas S. "Consider the Blessings," *Ensign*, November 2012, 86–89.

Monson, Thomas S. "Peace, Be Still," *Ensign*, November 2002, 53–55.

Monson, Thomas S. "The Sacred Call of Service," *Ensign*, May 2005, 54–57.

Monson, Thomas S. "The Spirit Giveth Life," *Ensign*, May 1985, 68–70.

Monson, Thomas S. "Tabernacle Memories," *Ensign*, May 2007, 41–42.

Nelson, Russell M. "Grow into the Principle of Revelation," *Liahona*, January 2021, 7–9.

Nelson, Russell M. "Revelation for the Church, Revelation for Our Lives," *Ensign*, May 2018, 93–96.

Nelson, Russell M. "We Can Do Better and Be Better," *Ensign*, May 2019, 67–69.

Nelson, Russell M. "What We Are Learning and Will Never Forget," *Liahona*, May 2021, 78–80.

Oaks, Dallin H. "Always Have His Spirit," *Ensign*, November 1996, 59–61.

Oaks, Dallin H. "Be Not Deceived," *Ensign*, November 2004, 43–46.

Oaks, Dallin H. "Good, Better, Best," *Ensign*, November 2007, 104–108.

Oaks, Dallin H. "How I Hear Him," *Invitation from the Prophet: Hear Him*. Accessed May 20, 2021, https://www.churchofjesuschrist.org/study/manual/hear-him-launch/how-i-hear-him-oaks?lang=eng.

Oaks, Dallin H. "Our Strengths Can Become Our Downfall," *Ensign*, October 1994, 11–19.

Owen, Stephen W. "Be Faithful, Not Faithless," *Ensign*, November 2019, 12–14.

Packer, Boyd K. "The 20-Mark Note," *Ensign*, June 2009, 2–6.

Packer, Boyd K. "The Candle of the Lord," *Ensign*, January 1983, 51–56.

Packer, Boyd K. "The Cloven Tongues of Fire," *Ensign*, May 2000, 7–9.

Packer, Boyd K. "Guided by the Holy Spirit," *Ensign*, May 2011, 30–33.

Packer, Boyd K. "Personal Revelation: The Gift, the Test, and the Promise," *Ensign*, November 1994, 59–62.

Packer, Boyd K. "Prayer and Promptings," *Ensign*, November 2009, 43–46.

Packer, Boyd K. "Reverence Invites Revelation," *Ensign*, November 1991, 21–23.

Packer, Boyd K. "The Spirit of Revelation," *Ensign*, November 1999, 23–25.

Parkin, Bonnie D. "Personal Ministry: Sacred and Precious," Speeches, *BYU*, February 13, 2007, https://speeches.byu.edu/talks/bonnie-d-parkin/personal-ministry-sacred-precious.

Pearson, Carol Lynn. *Beginnings*. Provo, UT: Trilogy Arts, 1969. First published 1967.

Perry, L. Tom, "That Spirit Which Leadeth to Do Good," *Ensign*, May 1997, 68–70.

Peterson, Lawrence R. "What limitations are placed on Satan? Can he put thoughts into our minds? Can he perceive our thoughts?" In "I Have a Question," *Ensign*, July 1984, 30–31.

"The Power of the Spirit in Conversion." In "Recognize the Spirit," *Preach My Gospel: A Guide to Missionary Service*, 98–99. Salt Lake City, UT: The Church of Jesus Christ of Latter-day Saints, 2004.

Pratt, Parley P. *Key to the Science of Theology*. 3rd ed. Salt Lake City, UT: Deseret News, 1874.

Rasband, Ronald A. "Lest Thou Forget," *Ensign*, November, 2016, 113–116.

Rasband, Ronald A. "Let the Holy Spirit Guide," *Ensign*, May 2017, 93–96.

Richards, LeGrand, "The Gift of the Holy Ghost," *Ensign*, November 1979, 76–78.

Richards, LeGrand, *A Marvelous Work and a Wonder.* Rev. ed. Salt Lake City, UT: Deseret Book, 1976.

Richards, Willard. Pocket companion, circa 1840. Church History Library, Salt Lake City, https://catalog.churchofjesuschrist.org/record?id=692b9f3e-0ea2-464b-9027-e6a4d8f7af06&compId=066ad7f1-4959-408b-8793-2b606bd3eb1c&view=browse.

Roberts, B.H. *A Comprehensive History of The Church of Jesus Christ of Latter-day Saints, Century I.* 6 vols. Salt Lake City, UT: Deseret News Press, 1930.

Romney, Marion G. "I would like to say a few things this afternoon about revelation . . . ," Conference Report, April 1964 (134th Annual Conference), 122–126.

Romney, Marion G. "Satan—The Great Deceiver," *Ensign*, June 1971, 35–37.

Romney, Marion G. "We Need Men of Courage," *Ensign*, May 1975, 72–74.

Scott, Richard G. "How to Obtain Revelation and Inspiration for Your Personal Life," *Ensign*, May 2012, 45–47.

Scott, Richard G. "Learning to Recognize Answers to Prayers," *Ensign*, November 1989, 30–32.

Scott, Richard G. "To Acquire Spiritual Guidance," *Ensign*, November 2009, 6–9.

Smith, Eldred G. "Decisions," *Ensign*, December 1971, 45–46.

Smith, Joseph, B.H. Roberts, et al. *History of the Church of Jesus Christ of Latter-day Saints.* 2nd ed. 7 vols. Salt Lake City, UT: Deseret Book, 1980.

Smith, Joseph, "Copy of a Letter from J. Smith Jr. to Mr. Galland." *Times and Seasons* (Nauvoo, IL), February 4, 1840.

Smith, Joseph. *Teachings of the Prophet Joseph Smith.* Compiled by Joseph Fielding Smith. American Fork, UT: Covenant Communications, 2002. First published 1938 by Deseret Book (Salt Lake City, UT).

Smith, Joseph F. *Gospel Doctrine: Selections from the Sermons and Writings of Joseph F. Smith.* Salt Lake City, UT: Deseret Book, 1986. First published 1919 by The Church of Jesus Christ of Latter-day Saints (Salt Lake City, UT).

Smith, Joseph Fielding. *Answers to Gospel Questions.* 5 vols. Salt Lake City, UT: Deseret Book, 1957–66.

Smith, Joseph Fielding, "The Sin Against the Holy Ghost." *The Instructor* (Salt Lake City, UT), October 1935.

Stevenson, Gary E. "Simply Beautiful—Beautifully Simple," *Liahona*, November 2021, 47–48.

Stevenson, Gary E. "Deceive Me Not," *Ensign*, November 2019, 93–96.

Stevenson, Gary E. "How Does the Holy Ghost Help You?" *Ensign*, May 2017, 117–120.

Taylor, John. *The Gospel Kingdom: Selections from the Writings and Discourses of John Taylor.* Selected, arranged, and annotated by G. Homer Durham. 4th ed. Salt Lake City, UT: Bookcraft, 1964.

Tyler, Daniel, contributor, "Recollections of the Prophet Joseph Smith." *The Juvenile Instructor* (Salt Lake City, UT), February 15, 1892.

Uchtdorf, Dieter F. "Come, Join with Us," *Ensign*, November 2013, 21–24.

Uchtdorf, Dieter F. "Missionary Work: Sharing What Is in Your Heart," *Ensign*, May 2019, 15–18.

Uchtdorf, Dieter F. "Of Regrets and Resolutions," *Ensign*, November 2012, 21–24.

Uchtdorf, Dieter F. "Your Potential, Your Privilege," *Ensign*, May 2011, 58–61.

Walker, Charles L. lyricist, and John Menzies Macfarlane, composer, "Dearest Children, God Is Near You," *Hymns*. Salt Lake City, UT: The Church of Jesus Christ of Latter-day Saints, 1948, 96.

Weaver, Sarah Jane, "Sister Wendy Nelson Shares Her Personal Witness of President Nelson's Prophetic Calling and Ministry," *Church News*, March 15, 2019, https://www.churchofjesuschrist.org/church/news/sister-wendy-nelson-shares-her-personal-witness-of-president-nelsons-prophetic-calling-and-ministry?lang=eng.

Whitney, Orson F. *Life of Heber C. Kimball, An Apostle: the Father and Founder of the British Mission*. United Kingdom: Scholar Select, 2016. First published 1888 by the Kimball Family (Salt Lake City, UT).

Wirthlin, Joseph B. "The Unspeakable Gift," *Ensign*, May 2003, 26–29.

Wirtz, S. Jill, "Check the Rear Door." In "Spiritual Promptings," *Ensign*, September 2008, 21.

Wolfe, Steven A. "Trapped Outside in the Cold." In "Spiritual Promptings," *Ensign*, September 2008, 19–21.

Woodruff, Wilford. "Discourse by Elder W. Woodruff, Tabernacle, February 22nd, 1857," reported by Geo. D. Watt. *Deseret News* (Salt Lake City, UT), March 4, 1857.

Woodruff, Wilford. "Discourse by Elder Wilford Woodruff, Delivered June 27, 1875, in the Second Ward School-house, S. L. City, at the funeral services of John Houseman, aged six years, and Willie Franklin, aged four years, sons of William and Ann Wheeler, burned to death at Wanship, Summit County, U.T., June 24th, 1875," reported by David W. Evans. *Deseret News* (Salt Lake City, UT), July 20, 1875.

Woodruff, Wilford. "Discourse Delivered by President Wilford Woodruff, at Springville, Tuesday Morning, March 5th, 1889," reported by Arthur Winter. *Deseret Weekly* (Salt Lake City, UT), April 6, 1889.

Woodruff, Wilford. *The Discourses of Wilford Woodruff.* Selected, arranged, and edited by G. Homer Durham. Salt Lake City, UT: Bookcraft, 1969. First published 1946.

Woodruff, Wilford. Journal, 1833–1898. Church History Library, Salt Lake City, https://catalog.churchofjesuschrist.org/record?id=400c3266-ede2-43cf-9a24-50153adebbeb&compId=8c4f3058-5de9-4278-be3c-7d02713f2dd2&view=browse.

Woodruff, Wilford, "Strange personal experiences—Preserved by the revelations and power of God—Incidents of a remarkable ministry—Great change coming over the earth—The work of God progressing," Conference Report, April 1898 (68th Annual Conference), 28–33.

Young, Brigham. *The Complete Discourses of Brigham Young.* 5 vols. Ed. Richard S. Van Wagoner. Salt Lake City, UT: Smith-Pettit, 2009.

Young, Brigham, John Taylor, Orson Pratt, Heber C. Kimball, George Q. Cannon et al. *Journal of Discourses.* 26 vols. Liverpool: F.D and S.W. Wells et al., 1854–86.

ABOUT THE AUTHOR

Loren Grant Dalton is the ninth of eleven children born to Leonard and Davida Dalton (and the youngest in a set of twins). He graduated from the Harvard Business School and has served as the president or CEO of five different companies.

One of Brother Dalton's greatest loves is missionary work. He has served in a full-time mission for over sixteen years of his life, as a missionary, mission president, or member of a mission presidency, both in the U.S. and Brazil. He married Annette Nielsen in 1984. They are the parents of four children.